Get your MAGIC Back

EMOTIONAL MASTERY FOR EMPATHS

COLETTE DAVENPORT

BADASS EMPATH UNITED

Cover art by Dragan Bilic at Upwork.

ISBN-13: 978-1-7339365-0-7

Badass Empath United
1103 Bentwood Road Austin, TX 78722
www.badassempathunited.com
www.colettedavenport.com

First Edition, May 2019

DEDICATION

This book is dedicated to my mom, Judith Kathryn Davenport, who has always seen me as magical. My greatest hope is to share my magic with others and honor the gifts you've given me. I love you mom.

CONTENTS

ACKNOWLEDGMENTS

I want to express deep gratitude for the following badasses who've helped make this book a reality. First are my coaches and teachers., Alicia Marie, Lauran Janes, and Jeffrey Van Dyk. Each of you taught me something extraordinarily valuable about life and business. Next up are my friends. You bitches are the best friends a girl could ask for. Allison Waddell, Joannah Hillebrandt, Julie Lehnis, Lauren Fielder, and Bradford Scott Walton, thank you for loving me just the way I am. Thank you to Melissa Yoder, Lynn Marie Morski, Rob Gregoire, Stephanie Hirsch, Chris Gatten, Fernando de la Garza, Riann McNaught, Jamy Squillace, Emily Rose, Christalle Bodiford, Amanda Evans Lang, Crystal Frazer, Kim West, Jesika Ford, Nadine Daniel, and Tiffani Marroquin for sharing your stories and for supporting this creative endeavor. To my fellow book babe, Crista Beck, thank you for the weekly pow wows, turning our dreams into reality. And last, but not least, thank you to Sean and Matt (last names will remain a mystery) for your roles in my life. I could not have made this without you.

Chapter One
HEALERS, FEELERS, AND MAGICAL PEOPLE

Have you ever wondered why you feel things so strongly? If you're like me, *a sensitive soul*, your emotions can dictate your actions causing you to shut down or strike back when shit happens. Biting your tongue and holding things in is not a productive way to be for people like us. Neither is erupting like a volcano, spewing angry molten lava all over the people we love.

We are healers, empaths, highly sensitive, *magical people*.

We are here to make a difference in the world. Whether you're an empathic momma raising conscious kids or a heart-based entrepreneur doing healing work *or both* it's vital that we deal with the deeply buried emotional 'wounds' so that we can do what we're here to do.

What I learned about my tribe long ago is that we are here to heal and return home.

I believe healing and returning home are the same thing.

Healing is an ongoing process, like a perpetual evolution. As we heal, we reintegrate parts of ourselves and restore a sense of wholeness in our hearts. The heart is where the soul 'resides' so healing is a returning home - to ourselves, our highest or spiritual selves.

Healing doesn't just take place in the body. In fact, the body cannot fully heal if the soul is still wounded.

You might even say, our world cannot heal if we, her people, are still wounded.

Our emotions, and the fight or flight response to situations that are not life threatening, are the keys to healing the soul wounds that we (*super feelers*) struggle with and suffer from year after year.

So what if you don't identify as an empath or a healer?

Will you still get something from this book? Heck yes!

The truth is we all have soul wounds that get triggered when shit happens. We all react the same way. We shut down emotionally or we strike back defensively. This book provides a simple process for dealing with the daily struggles and the deeper wounding so that you can **get your magic back.**

And if you *are* in my tribe of magical people making a difference in the world (or you want to be) this book is a foundational tool for overcoming the self-sabotage and secret addictions that keep you from being the badass you were born to be.

Heads up. I write for (and work with) people who are ready to come out of hiding. For too long we have numbed out and dumbed down to fit in. Our differences make us uniquely capable of serving others but we hang out in the shadows. Trying to be normal is a waste of time and energy. We have the power to transform. *It's time to own that magic.* The world needs us to show up, deal with our shit, and get to work making love, magic, and miracles the new normal. If your current normal is more *Struggle Boat* than *Love Boat* this book will be the lifesaver you've been looking for.

Stress, overwhelm, anxiety, depression, and addiction are not normal. But as a society we have been tolerating them as such. Some of us have even become so accustomed to living in these states that we don't know what it's like to be free. We don't have a reference point for feeling safe, supported, and fully satisfied. We only know life to be, in fact, a struggle.

We struggle with our health. We struggle with money. We struggle with love, especially self-love.

That just needs to stop. I'm here to make that shit happen.

Inspired to Write

The inspiration to write this book came as a result of four days in August 2018. A series of events that summer showed me the significance of the system I had created eleven months earlier.

Over the course of several years, I developed and taught myself how to heal my soul wounds and deal with the the day-to-day triggers that kept me sick, broke, and lonely. And while I was teaching the 4-step system to private clients (and getting results), I had not experienced it in action quite like that week in mid-August before.

Here's what went down.

I spontaneously drove to San Antonio to see my mom on a Sunday afternoon. This is a miracle in its own right considering I had only been back there one other time in the last 20 years. Home for me wasn't a happy place.

In fact, I prefer to describe it as, "the place I grew up". Home is Austin, where I've lived for 22 years.

But there I was excited to see mom and take her out for some Mexican food. My treat. I knew she was feeling the feels, too, since she's been the one *coming up to see me* for all those years.

So what changed? Mom got a new trailer.

The trailer I grew up in was like a coffin to me. I fucking hated it. When I graduated high school I moved out and never went back. In reality, the whole neighborhood was oppressive to my sensitivities.

Turning off of Highway 16 onto Twin Valley Road instantly triggered me. The first thing I saw was the icehouse my dad used to run. Then on the next block was a guy burning trash in his front yard -- because that's what you do in the country. Picture this. The entire street is lined with trailers in need of maintenance or demolition, broken down cars, various animals from horses to chickens to goats, and a lot of overgrown brush. It's pretty much a third-world vibe.

Mom's place is tucked away in the far back corner of the neighborhood. She loves that she can't see her neighbors, except her yay-bor Rosemary, from her one-and-a-half acre wildlife sanctuary. Yep, she's had her place designated as wildlife sanctuary where she enjoys birds, deer, the occasional wild boar, native flowers and her two dogs. She *loves* it there.

Now that the sarcophagus of a trailer I grew up in is gone, I can roll up and enjoy it with her.

Or I thought I could.

That Sunday as we left mom's place on our way to Don Pedro's, some of the neighborhood dogs came running toward my car. The car, with its fancy safety features, stopped just short of the pack of dogs. My mom says, "Just go, they'll move." Well, I couldn't and so we sat there for a minute til the dogs lost interest and trotted off. A little further down there were more dogs in the street. They weren't cared for. The look of them made me sick to my stomach. "Oh my God," I said, "how can these people let this happen?" To which my mom replied, "Just don't look."

Well, that set me off.

"Don't look?!?!"

"How the hell can you not see and feel their suffering?" Instantly, I was reminded of why I don't go back to the place I grew up. Being an empath made it nearly impossible to live in a home with an angry dad and an anxious and fearful mom. Even when I got out of the house and went for walks in the 'hood I felt pain. As a kid, I didn't know what it was but I do now.

That Sunday didn't turn out the way I intended.

I was triggered, which ignited the volcano of anger inside me and I spewed molten lava all over my mom.

I turned the car around and said some mean things, blaming mom for the misery of my childhood. "Just keep going" or "don't look" is how my mom deals with negative situations. I yelled at her for being in denial and her refusal to see my suffering. I was pissed. I dropped her off at home and drove straight back to Austin in a hellacious thunder-and-lightning storm.

As soon as I got home I ordered a pizza and sunk into the couch with my pups and movie to soothe myself.

The next day I woke up feeling guilty AF so I grabbed my

journal, a cup of coffee and set out to heal my pain and deal with my shit. I used the 4-step process that you will learn in this book to support myself. Anytime there's a big breakdown like the one I just shared with you, the situation isn't the issue. The soul wound is what needs your attention.

My mom isn't the issue.

The stray dogs are not the issue.

The trailer or the neighborhood or my childhood are not the issue.

My *soul wound* is what got provoked by these triggers. Without the wound there would be nothing to provoke.

This book teaches you what your soul wound is and how to heal it. From this place of understanding you're able to mend the relationships that are affected by your unconscious reactions.

After working through the system in my journal, I was able to communicate effectively with my mom. I called her and we *calmly* talked about what happened.

I apologized for my volcanic eruption and shared what I felt. I took responsibility for my half of the situation and pledged to practice patience in our relationship from that moment forward.

I also made the request that she put herself in my shoes and imagine what it was like for me as an empath growing up in a volatile environment. I shared my unique sensitivities and how energy and environment impact my emotional state. I let her know that "just ignoring things" or "just thinking positively" is not how I operate. I asked her to recognize that we process data (thoughts and emotions) differently and to please acknowledge that I feel things - all the things -

exponentially greater than most.

We hung up the phone that Monday morning feeling connected once again. Mom said she would come up to Austin the following weekend so we could have our mother-daughter time in a more soul-satisfying environment.

That "make up" weekend turned out to be one of the best weekends of my life.

The Tuesday following the San Antonio meltdown I was a guest speaker at the monthly meeting of the Polka Dot Powerhouse, an international women's networking organization. The title of my talk was, *Get Your Magic Back: Discover the Hidden Keys to Clarity, Confidence, and a Kick-Ass Life.* I didn't plan on telling the audience about what had gone down two days before, but to illustrate my 4-step system and how it works in real life, I got vulnerable.

I shared, with tears in my eyes, about growing up in a trailer with no A/C. I revealed the buried belief that I was "poor white trash." I talked about the anger I harbored towards my mom for not getting us out of that place, and how it erupted like a volcano. Then I taught the 4-step system that turned my breakdown into a breakthrough with mom in less than 24 hours.

In essence, I revealed my **soul wound** to a group of strangers, and the process I use to heal myself when shit happens.

The result? Tears. And not just mine this time. Several women thanked me for being real and raw. One shared a personal story with me she'd never told anyone. Another said she felt like I was speaking directly to her. Yet another woman in the audience, Melissa Yoder, asked me to speak at her women's retreat in January. We exchanged numbers, but that wasn't the most extraordinary thing that happened.

The next morning I got a text from Melissa.

"Good morning! My mom called me this morning angry about my 15 year old sister being a (insert negative low vibe word here). This is nothing new as I have a degree in child development. And I told her about your 4 steps and OH MY GOSH. We got off the phone with her feeling empowered and ready to work towards a solution! THANK YOU!"

A week later I got another text from Melissa.

"Just used your 4 steps to pull me out of a TOTAL meltdown."

So I decided to write a book that teaches my simple 4-step solution to the "emotional fight or flight response" that gets triggered when something that provokes our soul wounds happens, or as I like to say, *when shit happens.*

You can thank my mom, the Polka Dots, and Melissa Yoder for this.

Unpacking the Magic

Part one of *Get Your Magic Back* is going to teach you what your magic actually is, where it's at, and why you want to get it back. Of course, you probably already know why you want it back, that's the reason you picked up this book. But do you know your *soul's desire* - the deeper reasons why?

In the second part, we are going to set sail...in a boat. You're either in the Love Boat or the Struggle Boat. Regardless of which you're in now, you will be in the other at some point. Understanding where you're at, what to do when shit happens, and how to jump ship are invaluable to those on a personal growth journey.

In part three I'm getting vulnerable with you. I'll share my story to illustrate the ways in which our health, money and relationships *need* us to get our magic back. Use this section to bring your specific situation out of the shadows and into the light. *Reveal to heal.*

My 4-step process for healing at a soul level is the focus of part four. I'll teach you what a soul wound is, why you're not the only one who has one, and how to heal yourself. Hell yes, you can! Warning about this section: It's not pretty. It's ugly, it's disgusting, and if you're not in tears by the end of it, you're not doing it right.

The final part of *Get Your Magic Back* is about stepping out of the shadows and into the light...of your life. The three main reasons people like us struggle is because we lack 1) clear, healthy boundaries 2) an understanding of, and way to process, our emotions and 3) the ability to communicate effectively. This section is designed to help you put your insight into action.

There are no more excuses for staying sick, sad, broke or lonely.

When you get your magic back you will not only respond effectively (instead of react unconsciously) to situations that used to send you spiraling down into the black hole of suck, but you'll also have the power in your hands to create the kick-ass life your heart longs for.

Ready?

Let's make some fucking magic!

Chapter Two
MAGIC: WHAT IS IT? WHERE IS IT? WHY IS IT IMPORTANT?

What is Magic?

When I say magic I don't mean Harry Houdini and David Copperfield. David Blaine might be a better reference if you are under 40. The magic I'm talking about is the stuff inside you that makes life extraordinary, your power. In fact, the origin of the word magic describes exactly that. Here's a quick history lesson you might find interesting.

WORD	ORIGIN	MEANING
magh	Proto-Indo-European	might, bodily strength, power
mahan	Sanskrit	great
makhos	Greek	means, instrument
mogo	Old Church Slavonic	to be able
maeg	Old English	I can

The mystics of days past would use the word "magic" to refer to their wisdom. They meant their ability to recognize and understand the underlying forces of nature and the laws which govern them.

My favorite denotation of magic is, "the ability to change consciousness at will."

If you're like me, this resonates deeply. We are creators, manifestors, we are mystics who make magic on a daily basis. I've spent the last ten years on a soul healing journey, learning how to tap into my magic, and now I get to help others find theirs. Or as the book title suggests, get it back. Pretty cool.

So where is this magical power, you ask?

Where the Magic's at

It's inside of us. It's all around us. The universal law, "as within, so without" teaches us that what we believe and feel on the inside is reflected back to us in our individual realities.

I like to think about magic, as it relates to our personal power, being a quality of our spirit, essence, or soul.

I like to say the soul resides in the heart, of course that's more a symbolic than literal statement. You'll hear me speak a lot about things symbolically. I'm not a scientist, I'm a philosopher.

My proof that the **soul wound self-healing system** works is indicated in the robust nature of my life - I've gone from being sick, broke, and lonely to healed, prosperous, and having the time of my life! Other evidence of the success of this work is in the texts I get, like the one Melissa sent and these:

I wanted you to know how much the soul wound

work at the end of last year has impacted my life. The start of 2019 was a little unexpected but I've been able to just go with it because I'm now so content and comfortable with who I am. I didn't realize what the hard work we did would do for me until now. I was reflecting this past weekend and I felt that I finally just fit into this world. It's like I went from being a square peg in a round hole to the perfect fit. And with this "fit" has come a strong sense of inner confidence that is powering the way I now live. All choices now are made out of desire rather than desperation. It's the most freeing feeling I've had since I can remember. - Jamy S.

I am going to be very selective about who I date because I am finished settling, thinking that I'm not good enough for a great guy. - Lauren Z.

I was just sitting in a Salt Lake Coffee Shop this morning thinking about how appreciative I am to have you in my life & how nice it is on my 50th to truly know what I value in life. - Rob G.

Now, let's get back to *your magic*.

Your magic is in your soul. When we come to know ourselves at a soul level, inclusive of the wounds and desires, we have access to our magic. By the way, we were born magical AF.

For most of my life I denied my magic. I was distracted, disconnected, and disowning the best parts of myself. I think the payoff was that I didn't have to be responsible for my gifts. I could stay silent and 'safe' from ridicule - one of my biggest fears. But I always felt like something was missing. I never felt satisfied. I neglected my most precious gifts. My voice and ability to see and feel people was untapped for years.

I tried to be normal.

It wasn't until my early thirties that I began to recognize my desire for more than the mediocre life I was living. At that point I was introduced to Alicia Marie, a business and leadership development coach. She was the teacher I had unknowingly asked for. The way in which I learned about myself, though, was not normal. I think it was because she saw me as extraordinary. She sees all people this way. But that was the first time in my life that someone who had the skills to *help me see* - saw that in me. That was January 2007.

Since that earth shaking goal setting seminar I have dedicated my life to learning about myself, my gifts and how to use them for the greater good of humanity.

My soul's desire is to learn, heal, and grow and light the path for others doing the same.

That's my magic. What's yours?

Magic: a BFD

There's a reason I'm committed to helping you get your magic back.

For starters, I know what it's like to struggle with self-doubt and sabotage things so that I can't reach my full potential. That used to be my thing. My soul wound would land me in the dark hole of suck where I could claim depression and numb out with food, booze, drugs, television, hookups, and sleeping the day away.

Thank goodness for Alicia Marie. She not only helped me build a business, but she helped me break the unconscious patterns that were playing out year after year, keeping me disconnected and dissatisfied with my life. After the magical transformation I underwent working with her, I decided then and there I would help others get what I got.

Three reasons your magic is important are 1) Clarity 2) Confidence and 3) a Kick-Ass Life.

A connection to your soul's essence means clarity like you've never known before. No more self doubt. No more self-sabotage. No more secret addictions. *No more struggle.* You can be who you are, speaking your truth, surrounded by people who get you. You stop tolerating sucky situations, including the dead-end relationship, the job you hate, the chronic depression, and the credit card debt you're scared will never go away.

Life stops being something to deal with and starts being something you love.

When you're clear and connected you're confident and in control. You control your responses to situations, good and bad. You have authority over your emotional state and therefore you can choose how you want to experience life - even when things aren't going the way you want them to.

There was a time in my life where things definitely were not going the way I wanted them to. I sold a home I owned, paid off credit card debt and invested what was left in my intimacy coaching business. I hired an elite business coach, created my signature program, and bought all the online systems to market and sell my service to stressed out couples in sexless marriages. I worked harder and longer than I ever had in my life.

But guess what? The clients weren't coming.

Within a year I had maxed out the credit cards once again. The hustle and grind were *not* paying off. For months I was convinced if I just kept going the clients would surely come. There was a trickle where I needed there to be a flood. After months and months of pushing, I burned myself out and lost the hope for a bustling business that afforded me the lifestyle I dreamed of.

I remember thinking (more than once) I should just go back to being a call girl. Yes, escorting was a thing I did in my twenties, more about that later. I was tempted to give up and fall back into an unconscious pattern that neither served my soul nor my tribe of magical people. So what did I do?

I surrendered.

I let go of what I thought my business was supposed to be.

I gave up the hustle and grind and put my self-care first. I got connected to my soul-magic and trusted the Universe. Completely.

Then I took some bold and courageous actions.

I told my story of struggle, live on Facebook. I started writing articles for people like me, empaths and healers. I shared my systems for dealing with the black hole of suck, aka depression, anxiety, and addiction. I dropped the mask and opened my heart. All the walls came down. As a result of this level of self acceptance, my confidence soared. Despite the overdue bills and overdrawn bank accounts, I woke up every day with a *hell yes* attitude.

Faith, trust, and confidence allowed me to tap into my soul magic and share it with people vulnerably. I was no longer attached to how the people I am here to serve would show up. I no longer *struggled* with the situation of being broke.

I responded to it.

I told the truth. I came out of hiding.

I stopped letting the fear of rejection and ridicule run my life.

Being the source of our self-esteem gives us access to a creative state. We can accept the circumstances as they are instead of making the situation 'mean something' about us. Your worth is freed from the mess.

This is the freedom that lets you live a kick-ass life.

Almost instantly, I started getting emails and private messages from people who said, "I feel like you're speaking directly to me." My clients are now primarily empaths, healers, creatives and self-improvement seekers - not just couples in crisis. My business is booming and I feel totally aligned. I get to support some of the most magical people on the planet.

This feeling is fucking magnificent.

This is what I want for you. This is why it's important that **you** get your magic back.

Chapter Three
TWO BOATS

I came up with the 'two boats' concept while speaking at the Polka Dot Powerhouse meeting. I wanted the audience to identify where they were at that moment. Some women were in a solid place personally and professionally. They were riding the high vibe wave and enjoying life to the fullest. Others were feeling a bit less steady. A couple women confessed they were drowning under the stress of work, kids, marriage, health challenges and money issues.

My talk that evening was geared toward the women in the struggle-to-stay-afloat boat.

Those who were in the other boat, the Love Boat, would learn where the life vests were so they could support the people in their lives - and themselves when the time came. We're all in the Struggle Boat at some point.

So let's look at the two boats now.

The Love Boat

This boat is full of fun, romance, and satisfaction. Life on the Love Boat is a welcome adventure where everyone is successful, healthful and hopeful. It's high vibes and smooth sailing all day long.

We all want a ticket to ride.

If you're in this boat you probably have a lot to offer others. You might have achieved professional success that allows you to contribute to the lives of people you care about. You likely have a level of wisdom and understanding that guides your actions and gives you peace of mind no matter the circumstances.

Sailors on the Love Boat move along their path centered, grounded, and full of love - for themselves and life in general.

As I write this book, I'm sailing the high tides in the Love Boat. I'm feeling the good vibes and immense gratitude for the life I get to live. I've been riding this wave steadily for the last year and a half. I want to be clear, though, it has not been all rainbows and butterflies. Remember, there were months when I wasn't sure how I was going to pay my mortgage. I racked up overdraft fee after overdraft fee and my car payment was late. I maxed out my credit cards and had to borrow money from my mom to buy groceries.

The healing and transformation? **I was at peace the whole time.**

I gave up the fear and anxiety during the September of Surrender 2017. Prior to that, I was definitely in the Struggle Boat. Before I tell you about what that looked like, what there is to note is this. The circumstances of my life didn't change right away but what did was my experience of them. I was free of fear and anxiety. I had peace of mind and was able to focus on creating the reality I wanted.

Without the September of Surrender that would not have been possible.

Today I am more solid than I've ever been. My business is six-figure-robust. My extraordinary clients are healing themselves, falling in love, and launching new or revamping existing businesses. They have hope once again. I am surrounded by friends and colleagues who lift me up and hold me to my highest potential. I wake up with that *fuck yes!* attitude and I help other people do the same. This is the life I dreamed of for years. I am living it.

The coolest thing about being on the Love Boat is that I can point out where the life vests are for people who are struggling the same way I did. I can share my wisdom and experience to lessen the suffering of others. I can't do the work for you, of course, but I can shine the light on the path to peace, joy, and kick-ass satisfaction.

My hope is that once you find yourself, you too can shine your light brightly to lead the way for others who need you.

The Struggle Boat

Stress, overwhelm, anxiety, depression, and addiction are some of the symptoms of being in the Struggle Boat. Then there are the coping mechanisms like food, booze, tv, technology, sex, and social media. Last but not least are the secret saboteurs, Shirley and the Soul Wound. More about these later.

For now let's talk about the symptoms of the Struggle Boat.

Stress is an umbrella term we use to let each other off the hook. What I mean by that is, we are all unconsciously agreeing to avoid the real issues in our lives. Stress is actually unexpressed emotions. When we say, "I'm stressed" or "work is stressing me out" what we *aren't* saying is, "I feel powerless in my life" and "my hard work is being under-compensated and I'm secretly pissed about it but I can't say anything because I'd lose my job." Instead we feel stress. And instead of dealing with the root issue, we eat sugar and drink wine and watch reality tv to cope.

Overwhelm is the result of looking at too many things at once. In other words, *you* are not overwhelmed. Your *perspective* is overwhelming. There's a really easy way out of overwhelm. All you have to do is bring your viewfinder into focus. Look at what's right in front of you. Do one small easily achievable thing in a short amount of time. Check *one thing* off the list. And then do it again. And again until what you see is your ability to act consistently. That's how you will return to a state of "I got this".

Anxiety is ultimately the inability to embrace uncertainty and fear of the unknown. These things are part of being alive. While there are some things we can do to reduce the number of unknowns, they're never going away. You can put strategies in place to reduce your fears (and spend a lot of energy trying to maintain them) or you can dive into the fears themselves and take your power (and your life) back from them.

Depression is the dark night of the soul. Mystic priest Saint John of the Cross talked about his journey through despair to fuller holiness. Seeing depression as a spiritual hurdle reframes it. Judith Orloff M.D. says, "The 'dark night' speaks to your soul's development. It's not just about a biochemical imbalance or a neglectful mother, though these may be the provokers. It's a releasing of your ego's grasp on the psyche, permitting positive change that can prompt redefinition of the self. Since the period is profoundly unsettling, it's commonly perceived as 'darkness.' Mystics consider the dark night of depression not a negative, but a test of faith, an occasion for transformation."

Addiction is the uncontrolled need for another dopamine hit. And for empaths it's a hunger we need to feed. From mild, socially acceptable addictions like social media and iPhones to disruptive addictions like carbs and wine to destructive addictions like cocaine and heroin, we all struggle with something as we evolve.

Yes, you are addicted. We're all addicted to dopamine, the feel good chemical in our brains. So instead of coming up with more negative rhetoric, how about we deal with our addictions? Let's get conscious about what we're *really seeking* when we reach for the phone or a cig or a cookie or a line of coke. Otherwise, we're gonna stay stuck in the Struggle Boat for a long time.

The important thing to understand here is connection is the opposite of addiction.

We isolate ourselves to feed our addictions. This leaves us more lonely and in need of even more dopamine. Such is the cycle of suck. It does not matter if your addiction is to a substance, social media, a person's approval, achievement, or sex; the biochemical process in our brains is the exact same. So let's stop shaming one another for addiction and begin to accept that we are all addicted to something.

Why are we all addicted? Because we're disconnected *at a soul level.* To make matters worse, our constant self-sabotaging keeps us disconnected.

Shirley and the Soul Wound

I've written extensively about the soul wound. Maybe you've

even heard me speak on the topic. It is, after all, the 'soul' of my life's work. In chapter four I will teach you all about the soul wound and how to stop shutting down or striking back when you are triggered.

On the other hand, Shirley is the number one reason we repeatedly sabotage ourselves - even when things are going good.

Okay, technically Shirley has nothing to do with it. That's just the name I've given my negative, mean ass inner voice. We all have one. I suggest you name yours because, guess what, she's not you. You would never consciously berate and abuse yourself just for the fun of it. This unconscious aspect of being human can be corrected and even conquered. The trick is to catch negative Shirley when she's goin' off.

This bitch of an inner voice says things like, "Of course he ghosted you, look at you!"

She's great at keeping us small, scared, and silent.

Which of these is your inner bitch always reminding you of?

- "You'll never be the pretty girl so why even try?"

- "You're not rich, what makes you think you deserve a nice car (or home)?"

- "I wouldn't get too excited about that gorgeous guy/ girl, odds are they're gonna friend-zone you."

- "Ha ha ha, put those skinny jeans down right now, fatty!"

- "Don't call too much attention to yourself in the meeting, then they'll find out you're stupid."

- "Just stay home tonight, you're not going to meet anyone at the party like you."

- "What's the point in going to the gym, you're never going to lose weight."

- "You better not speak up, the relationship (or job) you're in is as good as it gets for someone like you."

- "Do I have to remind you of your past failures? Seriously, don't even try to set new goals."

- "What makes you think anything is going to be different now? You're the same loser you've always been."

The harsh reality is I could write an entire book on just the critical things *Shirley* says. She is a mean evil bitch!

Here's the thing though, *she doesn't mean to be.*

She's the voice of the soul wound. She represents the aspects of yourself that you've cast off. You've deemed something (many things, maybe) about yourself *unlovable.* These are the things you've decided are unacceptable, unworthy, ugly, dumb, useless, not good enough, broken, unmentionable, disgusting, horrible, and so on.

Again, we all have a soul wound and we all have the negative, critical voice as a result of the wound. We do not, however, need to live our lives buying Shirley's bullshit stories. When we heal at a soul-level we banish the bitch and become the conscious creator of the lives we truly want - and deserve.

Try this right now.

Name your inner bitch. Give her a name that you're comfortable saying, "shut the fuck up" to. I would avoid giving her an enemy's name because that makes it about someone else and this is about YOU. I chose Shirley not because I hated someone named Shirley. In fact, I had a best friend in elementary school named Shirley. I chose the name because I physically felt empowered saying the command, "Shut the fuck up Shirley!" the instant I noticed my negative self-talk secretly sabotaging my life.

This one thing alone will make a big impact on your ability to deal with challenging circumstances. When something is not going the way you want, you don't have to be a victim to the inner critic that insists you stay small, scared, and silent.

You do not have to shut down or strike back.

Chapter Four
WHERE'S YOUR MAGIC MISSING?

Check it out. Your magic can be missing in one of three areas at a time. Which doesn't mean the other areas aren't feeling it. They are. But we can only focus *fully* on one area at a time.

The three areas are:
Health
Love
Money

Each of these areas has different *symptoms* of the missing magic. I'm going to share some of the more common ones for people like us. Use this section to determine which area needs your attention the most right now. And trust me, you'll likely find your magic is missing in multiple areas. But for now, stay focused.

Health

STRESS.
There's positive-impact stress and negative-impact stress.

Positive-impact stress, called eustress, includes exercise, falling in love, travel, personal growth, healing yourself, giving a speech, and other things that make you uncomfortable in a good way. Negative-impact stress, or distress, can be acute or chronic. It can involve constant overwork, loss of a loved one, feeling misunderstood, doing work you hate, being broke, conflict with the kids, family members, or a spouse.

For my science nerds, I'll share an explanation of the stress cycle according to Dina Aronson, MS, RD from her article in *Today's Dietician*, "Cortisol - Its Role in Stress, Inflammation, and Indications for Diet Therapy."

Cortisol, (along with its partner epinephrine) is best known for its involvement in the "fight-or-flight" response and temporary increase in energy production, at the expense of processes that are not required for immediate survival. The resulting biochemical and hormonal imbalances (ideally) resolve due to a hormonally driven negative feedback loop. The following is a typical example of how the stress response operates as its intended survival mechanism:

1. An individual is faced with a stressor.

2. A complex hormonal cascade ensues, and the adrenals secrete cortisol.

3. Cortisol prepares the body for a fight-or-flight response by flooding it with glucose, supplying an immediate energy source to large muscles.

4. Cortisol inhibits insulin production in an attempt to prevent glucose from being stored, favoring its immediate use.

5. Cortisol narrows the arteries while the epinephrine increases heart rate, both of which force blood to pump harder and faster.

6. The individual addresses and resolves the situation.

7. Hormone levels return to normal.

The problem is most people think chronic stress is normal. It's not.

Chronic stress leads to anxiety and addiction. However, neither the stress, the anxiety, nor the addiction are the problems. Nope. They are all symptoms of an underlying situation I call your soul wound.

Unless the soul wound is addressed you can expect to be stuck in the stress cycle, shutting down or striking back at every turn.

OVERWEIGHT.

Excess weight is often the result of emotional stress. When stressed, we use food to feel better. It's called emotional eating and comfort food for a reason. For sensitive folks, food is one of the safest ways to numb out. Or is it?

We all know the implications of excess weight. I mean, who here *hasn't* at one point or another tried to lose weight?

If that's not you, congratulations, you have some kick-ass genetics.

For 97 million active dieters in the U.S. alone, however, excess weight is a real symptom of the *missing magic*. If this is your thing too, you know what it's like to feel trapped in the "never enough" cycle.

Never *thin* enough.
Never *satisfied* enough.
Never *loved* enough.

That last one, never loved enough, is the real issue here. You already know that deep down. You also know that the love you're seeking must come from yourself first. In other words, being overweight is a symptom of the missing **self-love** magic.

DEPRESSION.

If your magic is missing, you might be saying, "I'm depressed." You're not depressed. You are confused, and rightfully so.

Depression is a symptom of our unhealed soul wounds. When we add to that our high receptivity for other's wounding, we are up against some extra tough shit.

But guess what?

It's up to us to stop telling ourselves the bullshit stories that keep us sick, sad, broke, and lonely.

It's within our power to change how we feel. Getting the right kind of support is the key to overcoming our unique challenges. Normal approaches to health and healing don't work for us.

The reality is you have a soul wound that needs healing. We all do. What all soul wounds have in common is they make us feel worthless.

What goes with worthlessness? Powerlessness.

Our thoughts of being worthless and our feelings of being powerless are the source of depression.

If you're like I was, and those thoughts and feelings have taken over your mind and body, then I'm here to tell you you've forgotten who you really are. You're confused by all the nonsense messages stifling humanity. You're making your thoughts and feelings your identity. You're identifying as something you're not.

Let this be your reminder: You. Are. Magical. AF. And it's time to get your magic back!

ANXIETY.

Anxiety arises when we feel out of control. Empaths are often closet control freaks. We try to subtly control others and our environments so we can feel safe. Protecting ourselves from other people's energy is a common topic for empaths. We feel things so intensely that we become overwhelmed, leading to the anxiety that makes us control freaks in the first place.

I call bullshit.

Stop talking about the need to *protect yourself* and start standing in your power. Clarify (and honor) your boundaries and you won't need the 'bubble of light.'

There's a fundamental flaw in the guidance most well-meaning teachers offer to empaths and highly sensitive people.

The idea that we need to protect ourselves from other people's negative energy suggests we are incapable of handling it. It implies we are helpless victims. I don't buy it and neither should you.

That stance reinforces the story that we are "too sensitive" or "too much." It weakens our resolve and has us *hiding out* (in some fucking bubble) instead of coming out as the super-humans we actually are.

So what can we do to strengthen our will, build our confidence, and be the badasses we were born to be?

The first thing we must do is see ourselves as capable.

We cannot let society or our own fears dictate who we are and how we show up. We get to choose. We can sit down, stay quiet and play small or we can stand up, be bold and begin building the kind of life we truly want.

Once we have *this* powerful perspective we then can set healthy boundaries. Boundaries are one of the top three things we must set and respect if we are going to be the badasses we are born to be.

ON MEDS TO MANAGE.

Have you investigated the soul-level source of your health condition? Or are you mindlessly managing it with prescription meds?

You know you have the power to heal yourself and others, right? So why are you still trying to be normal?

Look, I get it. For years I took the meds - prescription and otherwise - to numb out and be normal.

If you're like I was, some of this may resonate.

- I used to feel helpless, hopeless, and out of control.

- I struggled with self-esteem most of my life. I was confused and depressed for years.

- I dropped out of college (to work as a call girl, thinking that would give me a feeling of control).

- I got sick (developed a visible lime-sized brain-stem tumor).

- I was afraid NO ONE would want me given my past AND this lump on my neck.

Then I got my magic back. I learned how to use my empathic abilities and healed myself. If you're an empath you have these gifts, too.

Vision - See the deeper (soul-level) wounds as the source of your sickness.

Intuition - Stop tolerating self-sabotage and build your self-esteem and self-trust.

Psychic Ability - Accept the thing that makes you different and stop trying to fit in.

Presence - Learn to love yourself unconditionally and let others be who they are. Give up trying to control everything.

Power to Heal - Recognize your unique and magical AF powers. I've used mine to heal my heart and now I'm on a path to transform my body. Stay tuned for *that* book.

The point is, if you're sick of tolerating a health condition, your magic is missing. To heal yourself, you gotta get your magic back.

SICK.

My wise and dear friend, Stephanie Hirsch, has a few thoughts about what it means to be sick.

> In my experience as a recovered bulimic, anorexic, laxative abuser, and depressed codependent, I found that being sick prevented me from even conceiving of my dream life. I didn't have the courage, confidence, or clarity to declare what I wanted; visualize that goal, and then hustle to make my

dream a reality.

When I asked my friends to tell me what it meant to them to be *well*, I got some really beautiful responses, starting with Stephanie.

> On the contrary, being well is a whole-body and mind feeling that I can achieve everything I dream of in my short term and long-term goals. I can manifest my future empire and have the energy and intelligence to create that empire every day whether it's a dream family structure, financial stability, or physical accomplishment when I'm "well". When I'm not well in my body, my brain suffers. And visa versa. True wellness is that moment where I literally heal my body and psychology with meditation and neuroplasticity: my mind propels my physical body to perform the way I want and need it to for the happiest and most purpose-satisfying life.

Fernando de la Garza shared his thoughts on being well, as well.

> To be well means loving yourself and being comfortable in your own skin. To enjoy life at its best without any remorse for the things you love to do. To give an effing big F%$$ on what people think about you and go for the dreams you always had. To have the courage to lift yourself up when things don't go your way and not let yourself down at any time. To wake up every day thanking the universe for another wonderful day of life. To forgive everyone that caused you pain and be in peace with them no matter how bad the pain was.

In my private Facebook group, Badass Empath, I polled the members asking what the number one frustration was, Health, Money or Love. Guess which the majority selected?

Health.

Whether we are struggling with mental, emotional, or physical health (or a combo thereof) we cannot sustain a satisfying life until we do something about it. Unless we reclaim our power, get our magic back, and stand up for the life we deserve to live, we will continue to struggle and suffer and contribute to the rapid decline of humanity. YOU HAVE THE POWER TO CHOOSE.

Please get responsible for your gift. Please, for the love of God, get your fucking magic back.

MY STORY: Lumpy

Before we go any further, I think it's important that you know how I got here and why this stuff matters to me.

It's spring of 1994 and I'm a super nerdy nineteen year old freshmen in college on academic scholarship that I received for being Valedictorian ...and I drop out to work as a call girl.

That was the most powerful and liberating choice I had made up to that point in my life.

As a teenager living at home I was not allowed to date and I had zero experiences with boys, sex, or my own sexuality. I wasn't allowed to talk to boys on the phone. I could only go to parties where parents would be there, even then I would have to come home early.

My dad was just trying to keep me safe, I know that, but instead of trusting me to make good decisions he threatened punishment and disallowed any activities that might lead to sex. Needless to say, I grew up with a lot of fear and shame around my body and sex.

Add to that, the challenges of being an empath and highly

sensitive person who was totally disconnected. And like most girls that age, I had major self-esteem issues.

While working as a call girl was an attempt at "power" as I was coming of age, it's simply a single circumstance, not the whole story.

My story is about soul wounds, self-esteem, and self-healing.

My story is about struggling with my sensitivities, absorbing my dad's anger and mom's anxiety and shutting down as a result. It's about feeling powerless and out of control.

My story is about numbing out to try and be normal, to fit in and not feel things so intensely.

Working as a call girl was a way to disassociate from my feelings - thinking this would make me feel in control, but it did the opposite. Instead, I felt what my clients were feeling. That pain and confusion is what made me to want to help people heal.

I also did a ton of drugs to "not feel" but, like the call girl thing, that's not the story just a coping mechanism.

That first semester in college was the first time I came out. I had been in hiding my whole life and I was done. I was done doing what everyone else wanted me to. I was done feeling ashamed of my body. I was done fearing sex. I was done feeling powerless.

I decided I was going to make ridiculous amounts of money, explore my sexuality, and feel in control of my body and life. And so I did.

It wasn't until much later that I discovered the underlying drive or what I call the "soul wound" that was directing my decisions.

At the time, I thought the attention of men was everything. Being paid to share my body seemed to give me the confidence I was missing. I felt I had the upper hand and could command these men to give me what I ultimately wanted - power.

What I didn't realize is that the exchange was not mutually empowering. Each of us was there to *take something* from the other. Later I also recognized there was an element of shame present (for both of us) in these transactions.

The most significant thing I learned as a call girl is that deep down we all have sexual fear and shame and self-confidence issues. Unless we heal these wounds they will continue to impact our decisions and unconsciously sabotage our lives.

Our wounds are usually hiding in the shadows and behind the mask, though, so it's tough to recognize them.

The men who hired me (and their wives) were not dealing with self-image, sex and intimacy issues in a healthy and productive way. Nor was I.

That's what lead me on a path to understanding how and why we are the way we are around sex, intimacy, body-image, communication, and relationship. And honestly, it's because my 25 year "obsession" with this stuff that I also know what actually works to heal our shame, overcome our issues, and have loving satisfying relationships and kick-ass lives.

Uncovering the soul wound and how it sabotages us is the basis for my body of work today. I believe this is the key to healing at a soul level.

My path to being an intimacy expert and master empath originated in my work as a call girl, yet the major transformation came when I got sick.

Being a call girl was an early catalyst for the healing work I do now, but it wasn't the critical point that lead me to actually heal myself.

My personal crisis came 14 years later. It was a life changing event.

In 2008, I developed a tumor on the nerve that goes from my brain stem to my tongue. I remember it like it was yesterday, I was sitting in the chair at the salon getting my hair done reading a *Women's Health Magazine*. Someone had written in to say, "I have a lump on one side of my neck that has been there for a few months. I'm not sick or symptomatic but it's not going away. What should I do?" The doctor responded with, "It could be something as simple as a swollen lymph node or it could be a serious condition like thyroid cancer. You should see your doctor immediately to get diagnosed."

I thought, "Fuck. This is exactly my situation." So I found a doctor and went for a diagnosis. After a needle biopsy resulted in an unclear pathology, which I was told was a good thing, the ENT recommended surgery to be safe.

In surgery, the doctors were able to determine the origin of the mass and decided to leave it intact since it was encapsulating the nerve fascicles deep within the 12th cranial nerve, which controls the function of my tongue. The prognosis was to wait and watch. Which I did.

In the first 3 years, I watched the lump grow to the point where I was avoiding eye contact with people. I didn't want to see their reactions when they saw me, or more specifically, the large lump protruding from just under my jawline.

Keep in mind, prior to this, I had always been outgoing. I modeled when I was younger, and I was a party girl in my twenties, all the while struggling with insecurities. My looks were my primary means of self-worth. Being *desirable* was what I thought mattered, where my value was. Yes, I am smart AF but my face and body was what brought me men and money. And love.

When this tumor showed up, my life as I knew it was over. And I thought that was the worst thing that could happen. It turns out it was THE BEST.

Lumpy made me want to hide my face.

One day I was at the grocery store and I saw an attractive man coming toward me in the spice aisle. Immediately I turned my head and averted my eyes to avoid making contact or being seen. As I strolled out of the spices I started to cry. Making eye contact, connecting with people, winking at hot strangers - that's my thing! I love that shit. It's my "spice of life" to create instant intimacy with people. And it was gone. I was totally dimming my light and hiding who I was. Again.

That's when I knew I had to take a serious look at myself and what I really wanted for my life. I didn't want to keep hiding, but I was ashamed, once again, about my body. And I felt powerless to do anything about it.

For as long as I could remember, I was ashamed of my body and my emotional sensitivity. I thought this made me a weirdo and I just wanted to be normal. The tumor caused me to confront all that.

So I got coaching. I devoured self-help and healing books from all the spiritual teachers, and I embarked on a year-long Tantra based spiritual development program. Over time and with a lot of high-level support, I came out on the other side of that crisis healed - mentally, emotionally, and spiritually. I'm talking NO MORE SHAME or embarrassment.

I awakened to the truth of who I am, and more importantly,

what I'm here to do.

My confidence has never been more rock-solid and the source of it is firmly rooted within me. Not men. Not money. Not status. No longer do I fear rejection or ridicule. No longer do I hide out or dim down. No longer am I struggling with sensitivities or insecurities. NO MORE.

My soul wound, "I'm an ugly disgusting waste of time," was the broken record playing in the background of my mind the whole time. And I finally saw it.

My crisis to gold moment is when I realized I had to share what I learned from all of this. I knew my magic had been unmasked! I could finally see how feeling powerlessness from the time I was a young girl, then working as a call girl, then having a tumor destroy my self-image were all part of the "training program."

I was ready to heal myself and come out of hiding, unmask my magic, and be the badass I was born to be - even with a fucking tumor on my neck.

The smartest and most meaningful thing I could do is take my whole experience of self-worth issues, along with the fear, frustration, anger, shame, and helplessness, and channel it to create something that helps other people **pulverize** those same internal issues.

I found my voice.
I no longer needed the approval of others.
I no longer needed to be wanted or desired.
I no longer needed to be normal.
I could be ME.

I am here to show the way for my fellow empaths and highly sensitive people to do the same.

Get Your Magic Back is my way of helping other wounded healers, empaths, artists and creatives turn their sensitivities into superpowers and be the badass you were born to be.

If you're not currently dealing with any health issues - great! My biggest wish for you is that you do not wait until you develop a tumor (or something similar) to begin healing yourself.

Love

SEXLESS MARRIAGE.

If you're an empath with zero sex drive and zero sex life this is for you.

A stressful situation is the likely *catalyst* that shut down your desire for sex. But your programming is probably the ongoing cause. Compound that with your empathic sensitivities and you end up living more like roommates with your partner than lovers.

It's not your body... It's your beliefs.

Specifically, what I mean is it's *your beliefs about yourself and the circumstances* that are creating the undesirable situation called a sexless marriage.

The catalyst, or what I call a triggering event, may be what you're focused on. Thinking, "When I can get *this* under control *then* I can start looking deeper into what's going on with me."

Sorry, boo, but you got it backwards.

I know it feels like you can't possibly put yourself first right now. The challenge is real. But the way to overcome *this challenge* is to put YOU at the center of your life. Stay with me.

The reality is there's a deeply held belief about yourself that is in need of healing. You could call this your "programming," I call it a *soul wound*. The good news: this is the center-point of your spiritual journey.

The job of the soul wound is to help you evolve.

The thing about being an empath is we get good at rationalizing our feelings so we can cope and "survive." Our heightened sense of subtle energy and emotions are often seen as a setback. However, the same sensitivity actually helps us be great healers and helpers. You're in the teaching, wellness, health/healing or human rights field, right? Yep.

Another drawback is that our sensitivities can blind us to the deeper issues lurking within.

How?

- We have normalized feeling stressed and anxious. So we don't recognize there's a problem.

- We have developed extraordinary coping skills. We can deal with the day-to-day stuff pretty well (hello, self-care!) but this "symptom soothing strategy" takes our focus away from the source of the situation.

- We think there's something fundamentally wrong with us or that we're "cursed." This is mostly unconscious but it's there. You know what I'm talking about.

When there's a crisis, empaths shut off all unnecessary parts of ourselves so we can deal with the event causing chaos. The first thing to go is our sex. Buh-bye sex drive.

Stressful event = sexual shutdown.

This makes sense biologically. If you're being chased by a man-eating saber-toothed tiger it's not helpful to be horny. You need that sexual energy to run like hell to safety. Thanks nature, for our autonomic nervous system!

The problem comes when you're safe from danger and you're still in 'fight or flight' and still shut down sexually.

You might have chronic stress to blame or you might not know how to break free of your patterned shutdown behaviors. Or it may have been so long ago that you saw yourself and your partner as a sexual being that you've buried your hot button.

No matter which of these is true, the very first thing to do is get a grip on your perspective. The situation is not the issue; your soul wound is.

Girl, get your *sex magic* back. You are more than a physical body with a brain meant to act out each day from a practical perspective. You are also an emotional, spiritual, and sexual being.

Empaths have an advantage over everyone else when it comes to these "other bodies" We feel them intensely but we aren't listening to then intently. Master your sensitivities and watch the magic and miracles show up.

GIVEN UP ON FINDING LOVE.

Too many of us who struggle with our wounds and self-sabotaging stories fall into this category. This shit is lonely and depressing. If you're here, what you've really said is, "I give up on *me.*"

You have nothing but your beliefs about yourself to blame. It's not you. It's your beliefs. It's not your body. It's not your past or having five kids. It's not that you're too busy or too broke to date. You don't think love is in the cards for you.

Are you seeing a pattern here?

If you're not making love it may be because you're mind fucking yourself instead.

To get your magic back you must first believe in yourself. Believe it to see it. That may be hard when you have a mountain of evidence that "proves" you're unworthy of your deepest desires. Or that love is hard and will only hurt you.

If you want it to be different bad enough you will commit to seeing yourself and your future free from the past. A new you awaits when you do the work to heal at a soul level.

If you really really want to give up on something, give up on the belief that you can't find or have love.

My clients, every week after their calls, answer the following question, "What thought or belief are you willing to give up in order to achieve your goal?" So I ask you right now, what is your response? Write it down and commit to giving up one of your limiting beliefs in this very moment.

SETTLED FOR LESS OR RESIGNED.

If you're in a relationship that is not feeding your soul or igniting your magic, you have settled. Now, it goes both ways. You being resigned and thinking, "this is as good as it gets" makes you half-ass how you are showing up in your relationship. So of course, it's not likely your partner sees the spark in your eyes.

We get back what we put out into the world.

Are you giving unconditional love to yourself and your partner? Or is your love and affection given only when something is done for you. If you're playing the tit-for-tat game you will never be satisfied.

Let's start with you giving yourself the unwavering love you want to get from your partner. Who would you have to be to give yourself that? What qualities would you need to embody to be the woman who loves herself fiercely? The woman who does not settle for anything less than extraordinary? (This would be a great time to utilize the journal at the back of this book, btw.)

Now look at exactly what you're putting out into the world. The people in our lives are always mirroring back to us what we feel about ourselves inside.

Consider that if your partner is distracted and giving attention to the television or work more than he is to you then *you are distracted from your values.* There may need to be an assessment of your values and some communication concerning them with your partner.

What are your top five values in relationship?

How are you honoring and communicating them?

What are you keeping quiet about that you need to reveal?

Where are you settling for less than you deserve?

How could you show up fully for yourself today, and shift your thinking about what you're putting out there?

LONELY

When our magic is missing in Love, life can be lonely AF. This is no way to live. If this is what you're struggling with, sis, it's time to get your fucking magic back. Whether you are single or in a relationship, being lonely sucks. We need to feel connected in order to thrive.

In a 2015 study of more than 3 million participants, researchers at Brigham Young University found that increased social connection is linked to a 50 percent reduced risk of premature death.

According to another study from the British Red Cross, over nine million adults in the U.K. feel lonely. That's about 1/5 of the country's population! Loneliness is increasingly being considered a hazard to human health comparable to obesity and smoking.

Too often we hide our loneliness because we think it is a shameful thing. Especially, if we are in a relationship. We'd rather suffer in silence than speak up about the emotional abandonment that we are tolerating.

When I asked my social circle to, "Tell me about the time you were lonely," Lauren Fielder said, "I have been the loneliest inside of dysfunctional relationships." To which Caroline Rose replied, "I agree..I was the loneliest in my marriage. The dysfunction and hurt kept me isolated."

Chris Gatten added:

> I think when lonely happens, it's because I feel like no one knows me truly in a particular moment. No one would understand why my pain was so deep for a seemingly small transgression, or no one knows my history enough to know my inside jokes from childhood.
>
> A sense no one sees you authentically, those are moments I find myself lonely.
>
> Sometimes though, this smart inner voice reminds me at those moments that I Myself am present to appreciate what otherwise might go unseen. I count

as a witness to my existence too, even if only for my lifetime. If I feel like no one else is seeing me, at least I can see myself. Being my own witness has been crucial to some hard times in life.

In 2018, the U.K. appointed a Loneliness Minister, Tracey Crouch, to help combat the country's chronic loneliness problem. In the U.S. the government has yet to step in but loneliness is considered an epidemic that is contributing to the general health crisis. I believe the crisis will be cured when we each address our unique soul wounds.

The science tells us that when we're separated from others, we find ourselves in a mental stress state called "fight or flight." Being around other people provides a sense of safety and security that stifles this stress state and decreases the perception of loneliness. When alone, or feeling alone, people subconsciously sense that they must be more aware of threats in the environment, so the body prepares to deal with them through the stress response.

Stress triggers a cascade of hormones that orchestrate all kinds of changes in the body. Have you ever experienced a racing heart, muscle tension, or quickness of breath because of stress? Yep. All of that is designed to prepare us to fight a threat. But the body doesn't know the difference between a real threat, like someone chasing you or an approaching work deadline, or a perceived one, like feelings of loneliness.

All research studies aside, I know a thing or two about being lonely in love. In my experience, the loneliness always comes after the emotional abandonment.

MY STORY: Naked, Abandoned, and Alone. My Worst Fear Realized.

I was thrust out of a dream this morning at 5:55 a.m. gasping for air. As I came to, I realized I was not running down the street barefoot desperately calling after him, but safely tucked in my bed having the recurring nightmare that surfaces when I give my heart to a man.

In last night's version of the dark dream, I was ruthlessly dumped by John. He was secretly seeing someone else, and although I knew, I silently hoped his feelings for me would sway his heart in my direction. Instead, I woke just the door was swinging shut.

The first thing I noticed were the empty hangers in the closet. Then I saw the bathroom was no longer cluttered by his many medications and manly things on the delicate shelf. In the thirty seconds or so it took me to realize what happened, I had forgotten I was completely naked and only knew I had to go, now, run after him.

Maybe I could still catch him?

Maybe I could convince him to stay?

I was running, searching, breathless and hopeful at the same time.

He was gone. Disappeared.

I was once again naked, abandoned, and alone. My worst fear realized.

The fear runs deep.

I'm not 100% certain if the memories are real but I've had vague visions of my dad visiting a woman who wasn't my mom when I was in preschool. What I do know for sure, is he wasn't there for me, mom, or Clayton emotionally.

I honestly don't know if they ever experienced the brutal

impact of his emotional neglect or if they're such "logical people" that they rationalized and repressed the abandonment. You'd have to ask them.

I, however, felt it deeply. And apparently I still do.

The worst thing that can happen to an empath is emotional abandonment.

My dad was physically there but emotionally vacant. Well actually, not vacant as much as volatile. His emotional range hovered between anger and apathy. I remember being stressed out and tense, wanting to hide most of my later childhood. I say 'most' because early on there were more good days than bad.

I loved my dad. I was a daddy's girl. He taught me to drive a tractor, to use tools, to think strategically. He picked me up from elementary school and bought me a DQ ice cream cone every day. He brought me to work with him where I watched him run his business and build relationships with customers. I credit him with my desire to be an entrepreneur. And my love of DQ ice cream.

I idolized my dad.

Ray was a charismatic, witty, popular dude with a big personality and stature to match. He was admired and respected -- most of all by me. I felt safe with my dad. His motto was, "Davenports never lie, cheat or steal." I could depend on my dad.

THE COUGAR

That all changed at some point. I can't pinpoint exactly when. It could be the time I got in trouble for singing John Cougar-Mellencamp's song, *Hurt So Good*. I was at dad's office playing with my Barbies under the desk (my little playroom) when the song came on. I loved to sing. Still do, although I feel super self conscious about it. Possible side effect? Who knows.

So here I am, a third-grader singing a song and playing make believe when dad calls my name -- in that voice. The voice where I knew something was wrong. I crawl out from under the desk walk over to him and timidly ask, "Yes daddy?"

He takes a long drag from his Salem menthol and before exhaling asks, "Make what hurt so good?"

I thought for a moment, twirling Barbie's blonde hair around my uncertain fingers, and said, "Love?"

Dad: "What do you know about love?"

Me: "That it hurts?"

Dad: "What does he mean when he says love?"

Me: "When two people are together like you and mom."

Dad: "And what to two people who love each other like mom and me do?"

Me: Starting to cry, "Yell at each other?"

Dad: Takes another drag then stubs out the cigarette, "You know better than that. Stop that crying."

After a hug and using his hankie to wipe my tears and blow my nose he sends me back to play.

I know now that he was investigating what I might know about sex at such a young age. I knew nothing, only that I like the song and singing out loud. But as I sat, shaken, in my little nook under the desk on the floor I felt less safe.

THE BEAR

Maybe my trust in dad was damaged due to the time he disciplined Clayton, my older brother, by taking away his teddy bear.

I wish I could remember what Clayton did to piss off my dad, but it seems he was always mad about something so who knows what this time was about. Clayton might remember.

All I recall was Clayton's bear was not only taken away but sent away on a Greyhound bus.

I suppose that was the way to really make it hurt because it was final. Teddy wasn't coming back. This was a serious punishment. Clayton was so upset. We were both crying and dad was talking about how Clay brought this on himself.

I just remember thinking how cruel it was to take away the thing he loved so much. I felt for my big brother and I lost faith in my father as a protector.

I'm guessing my dad felt remorse after he sobered up because a week later Teddy returned from his road trip and all was right again.

All except the trust I had in my dad to love us unconditionally.

THE AWAKENING

Maybe I stopped being daddy's girl because of all the times my mom woke me up in the middle of the night to tell me that we were leaving. She and dad would fight a lot when he came home drunk.

Every time I would go to bed before my dad came home I would be afraid of what would happen later. More often than not he would come home, making a bunch of noise, waking up my mom to fix him something to eat and the argument would ensue.

Then at some point it would get so bad that my mom would threaten to leave and come in my room to get me dressed. Sometimes we made it all the way out to the car before dad would convince her to stay. On occasion we would drive around while my mom cried and I tried to soothe her, feeling her pain, being angry at my dad and confused by the whole situation.

This pattern played out so much I can only imagine how my feelings of safety and certainty and trust in my dad would wither away with each occurrence.

The truth is I don't know at what point I stopped trusting my dad. I do know my feelings about the man I loved and admired were forever altered as I grew up.

Sadly, that lack of trust carried over into every single one of my relationships since. That's 40 fucking years of trust issues and fear of abandonment.

THE FIRST BOYFRIEND

Joe was the first guy I dated and had an ongoing sexual relationship with. I was 19, had my own apartment, and was a freshman in college. We met at Castle Golf and Games, the job I got the summer after high school.

Joe and I would go to parties, hang out at my place or his parents place, and do stuff with his friends. I felt special.

One time we were at his friend's place and there was a secret conversation happening that made me very uncomfortable. I got the impression Joe had another girlfriend and his friends were joking about how if she found out about me all hell would break loose.

She found out.

Then she found my apartment.

Roxanne what is a twenty-seven-year-old fiery redhead who had a temper and was in love with my man.

I was very much intimidated by this older woman. And yet I was obsessed with not losing Joe. Although I did not feel safe I was still trying to hold on. And the trust issues? Well they were in full blown attack mode.

One night Joe was at my place and said he was going to take out the trash for me. Acts of service? I'm into it. Only, he didn't come back.

I never saw Joe again.

THE FIANCÉ

Sean and I met at the Ritz, an old school Austin dive bar on 6th Street. We had a summer fling that turned into an 8 year long relationship. The long and short of it is this; we started out with a lot of time, a lot of freedom, a lot of play, and a lot of emotional investment in one another and then we became focused on other things.

We were at an age when it was time to start thinking about a future, a career that would provide security. We went from both of us working from home to each of us working in completely different worlds.

His work was monopolizing his time. He knew it but could not or would not do anything about it.

And while there was not another woman involved I eventually felt like an option in his life and not a priority.

I felt emotionally abandoned.

My feelings went unheard until I stopped expressing them. The thing about feelings is, they don't go away when we try to numb them, they just get repressed or in my case, compressed into a lime-sized tumor on the nerve that controls my tongue.

Lumpy arrived on the scene a few months after I broke up with my fiancé, Sean.

We now believe the lump is an encapsulated infection, a result of the Epstein-Barr virus, aka *the heartbreak disease.*

THE LAST BOYFRIEND

Three years after Sean and I parted ways, I met Matt. He reached out to me on Facebook. We had a blind date on a Saturday in December. Two weeks later I was meeting his friends and family at their annual holiday party.

The first year of our relationship was exceptional. Even though Matt lived four hours away, we rapid and deeply built a connection that was intended to be lifelong.

In 2012 I went to doctors at MD Anderson, the premier cancer treatment hospital in the country. Although my tumor was not cancerous, I believe this experience changed the way Matt saw me -- as a fragile and sick woman.

I, no doubt unconsciously, played into the role of needing to be taken care of. It would assure he would not leave me. Matt is fiercely loyal.

After another year and a half of a long distance relationship, I moved to Houston to live with my man. But Matt was struggling with his purpose. He was not fulfilled with his work. He wanted his efforts to have meaning and impact, something I admire greatly. I encouraged him to follow his passion. We moved back to Austin, he took a significant pay cut and committed himself to a start-up he believed in.

He was seldom home after that. And when he was, he was working. Our intimate relationship suffered and the stress increased. I shut down. Once again, I felt emotionally abandoned.

The relationship ended and Matt moved out over the Christmas break 5 years after our first date.

In the last three years since the break up with Matt, there has been no growth of the tumor. I've given my attention to this aspect of myself that altered the course of my entire life. I started to love and accept myself and heal the wounds related to my heart. To Men. To trust, and to my self-worth.

I don't think that would have been possible in the circumstance of our relationship.

Two weeks ago I fell in love again.

I didn't even realize it until I woke up from the dream this morning. I couldn't understand why I was so affected by this man and his actions.

On the surface this makes no sense. We only met six weeks ago. We only had sex once. How could my heart be so *involved?*

This morning I saw behind the curtain. My dreams always awaken a deeper truth.

We were emotionally entangled as much as our bodies were that night and I opened my heart to him. I felt safe and seen and I said yes to his penetrating presence.

I took him in and held him tight. We couldn't get any closer physically -- and for me, emotionally.

I don't separate physical intimacy from emotional, they are

merged in my experience.

It had been years, almost 8 to be exact, since I felt this state of ecstasy and connection. It was a sexual-spiritual-emotional freedom. I was welcome to be me, all of me.

It was I who abandoned my armor, the protective gear I had assembled around my heart to keep it safe from the careless treatment of men.

A dormant part of me came alive again that night. I was turned on like a high-voltage battery, feeling the vibes for days after. Yet in the days after I noticed a shift in his attention. It wasn't what it had been in the weeks prior.

My deep wounds were triggered. I felt like an option and not the priority I once did. I said as much. Yet nothing changed. No conversation about my feelings was invited.

So there I was, naked, emotionally abandoned, and alone. My biggest fear realized. Again.

My trust shattered. My heart discarded. My feelings, "too much."

My hope in men and love and being wanted as I am - *with all the feelings* - disappeared just like his texts and calls and interest in me.

Then I woke up.

I realized this was just another opportunity to heal and restore wholeness to my heart.

I think that's my lesson in life. With men, I keep having my trust and heart broken to varying degrees.

The thing to heal is not my body but my heart. This

tumor is the result of repressed and compressed emotion from the heartbreak that has repeatedly happened since I was daddy's girl.

My job is to trust that I am safe and loved now and always.

These men who would disregard my gift, who could not fathom the depth of my emotional capacity to love, would teach me to love myself.

So how could I not love these men? How could I not continue to keep offering my heart completely to someone?

My greatest gift is the love I have to give. My heart is as deep and vast as the ocean from which it came.

My biggest wish is to share it fully and with absolute trust that I am worthy of being received the way I am.

Today I stop chasing and searching. I'm giving up the fear of being abandoned and alone. I'm setting free the wound that would whisper, "You're too much, Colette."

I trust I am perfect as I am. I trust my man will see my sensitive soul and flaws and fall in love with all of it.

All of me.

Money

HATING YOUR JOB.

I talk with empaths everyday who are working a 9 to 5 and hate it. It zaps their energy and sucks the life out of their soul. Staying stuck at a job you hate will def make your magic disappear.

If this is you and you know you need to make a change for your health but are scared shitless about what it would do to your wealth, you are not alone. There are a few things you can do to support yourself that range from strategic quitting to training your colleagues how to work with you and your sensitivities.

My client, Dr. Lynn Marie Morski is a strategic quitting evangelist. She is a physician, attorney, and lifelong quitter. As a podcaster, speaker, coach, and author she helps people carve out successful lives through strategic quitting. Lynn Marie came to me because she wanted to do less doctoring and more private coaching. We designed a program that she could market to her ideal clients through her podcast and speaking gigs and get paid well for her expertise in strategic quitting.

She also has a great book that will support you if you're just now thinking about leaving your soul-sucking job. Check it out:

Quitting by Design: Learn to use Quitting as a Tool to Carve out a Successful Life.

Thousands of self-help books have been written to tell people to live their best lives, without necessarily addressing the fact that making major life changes almost always requires quitting one thing and starting another.

This pain point – the quitting itself – is often the barrier to change. Many avoid quitting because they fear the unknown. Will they find another career or relationship? Will their new path provide financial stability? Will friends and family question the decision to quit? Will society see them as quitters?

These questions generally go unaddressed. But that's where Quitting by Design comes in – its sole focus is to help people through their quits successfully so they can proceed with their transformations. It's a step-by-step guide that takes readers from deciding if there's something they should quit all the way to preparing their health, finances and relationships for a quit, and it helps them conquer any fears that may pop up along the way.

You can find Lynn Marie at www.QuittingByDesign.com and her book at Amazon and Barnes and Noble.

STRUGGLING TO SURVIVE AS AN ENTREPRENEUR.

If your money magic is missing it probably feels like you have few to no options, especially if you're an entrepreneur. You're likely stressed and using coping mechanisms like food, booze, and social media to calm the inner chaos.

You might've gone *all in* on some high-end coaching, the Facebook ads training, a webinar strategy course, and so on. If you're buying the "hustle and grind" way of entrepreneurship and it's not working, there are some specific reasons why.

Here's how 'hustle and grind' kills the empath's spirit and sabotages our success.

For empaths, it all starts with a deep feeling inside us, a 'knowing'. We feel the pull to create a particular body of work. It has meaning. It serves the greater good. It has the potential to make the kind of money we need to live the kind of life we dream of. We feel so much passion, we can't *not* go for it.

After all, it is our purpose.

We begin devouring all the information we can. Like a mermaid, we dive head-first into the warm welcoming waters, the swimming pool of learning. We invest in developing our skills, honing our message, and embracing processes for online marketing and sales funnels.

We get certified and licensed and join professional groups.

We purchase programs that teach copywriting and content creation. We sign up for seminars and webinars to learn the systems and formulas to succeed as entrepreneurs.

We implement the systems, formulas, and funnels. They don't work. We fail. We fall short. We try again. And again. We hire the experts to help us. We are pushed to our limits. We expand those limits and keep going. We use all our resources.

We fear running out of money.

We have to start 'dealing with reality.'

We keep going, but now we're operating from fear instead of love.

We find ourselves stuck in fear, in the 'dominant' mindset, (make it fucking happen!) even though *we know* we create best from love, in a 'flow state'. How many of us operate from force rather than power?

For Empaths, falling into the fear state where force and control are the norm is the surest way to sabotage success.

We question ourselves, our abilities. We then work harder and more diligently than ever (to prove we *are* capable), staying up late, sacrificing our self care, sinking into isolation.

We cope with the stress by using feel-good substances like caffeine, nicotine, sugar, and alcohol.

We withdraw from our relationships. Why? Because deep down we have triggered our soul wound, "I'm not good enough," and we sure as hell don't want *them* to see that. We've spent our whole lives avoiding the pain of rejection and ridicule.

But here we are again sick, broke, and lonely. Sound familiar?

What once was vision, passion, and inspiration turns to self-doubt and Spirit-killing negative thoughts (or what I call the mind-fuck).

We start thinking, "Am I so broken that I can't figure this out?" "Am I delusional?" "Are my dreams too big?" "Should I just give up and get/go back to/stay at a normal job?" WTF?!

Here's the thing about us. Feelers are leaders, not followers.

My good friend Emily Rose says, "Fuck the formula."

What that means is, for entrepreneurs like us, the typical systems and strategies lack the flexibility and freedom required to work our magic. Emily and I have both discovered what actually works for gifted, purpose-driven entrepreneurs.

Not only is Emily a friend, a colleague, and a fellow empath, she is someone who has triumphed over repeated failures and a deep depression. Today she is a best-selling author and self-actualization coach.

She is a badass.

Here's how you can be a badass empathic entrepreneur, too.

SURRENDER
The biggest gift you can give yourself is an internal shift to love, where true power resides.

- Give up trying to control things - this comes from fear and force. It does not work for us.

- Replace the routine you're struggling to maintain with

a ritual that you love. Focus on self-care.

- Say 'Yes' to yourself and 'No' to others. The truth you seek is inside you - stop looking externally.

- Tune into the vibration of Love. That frequency is creative and magnetic.

- Remember your magic. Learn to master it and let go of the rest.

From this place of surrender emerges a new awareness, trust, POWER, greater truth, and confidence. You have access to the wisdom and insight you need to take inspired action. You are coming from a place of Love.

> Do the thing and you will have the power.
> — Ralph Waldo Emerson

OUR POWER

As empaths, our ability to harness and amplify positive/ productive energy is our gift. It's what there is to get responsible for. When we are stuck in hustle and grind, we are far from our power - Grace and flow. Surrender is the path to power. In power, we are manifesting effortless results.

These results come from things like:

- Clarifying and committing to our purpose

- Alignment with Source energy through self care

- Designing enhanced environments that set us up for success

- Trusting our magic - not giving a damn what other people say

- Utilizing a system that takes our sensitivity into account, turns it into our superpower

- Understanding and healing our soul wounds

- Confidently communicating our needs to others

- Having an inspired strategy to wake up and work on that comes from a place of love and power

When we fall into the hustle and grind we fall out of alignment with our Source energy and superpower. Things get foggy so we follow the popular formula for success. We sacrifice ourselves, our relationships, and our magic while we're struggling to achieve success.

If you're here, the thing to do right now is SURRENDER.

Love and Power are creative and magnetic. As an empath, your ability to harness and amplify that energy is your gift. This is your magic, my friend. It's what there is to get responsible for. From the place of power, new awareness, trust, greater truth, and confidence can emerge. You will work, then, from an aligned state of Grace and flow. You will create results with effortless ease. You will manifest the money, the people, and the situations that support your deepest desires and dreams. *You will get your magic back.*

IN DEBT UP TO YOUR EYEBALLS.

When my money magic was missing, I wound up living on credit cards, borrowing money from my 80 year old mom, and wondering when my electricity was going to get cut off. It sucked. Real bad.

The year before I decided to go all in on my coaching and speaking business I sold the home Sean, my ex, and I lived in for six years. I also broke up with Matt, my then partner, who was taking care of us financially. Selling the house was not only symbolic of some serious surrender on my part - letting go of the men I loved - it was also a means to pay off my credit cards and invest in my business. A fresh start.

Within a year of doing so, however, I was back to using the credit cards to buy Facebook ads, webinar hosting platforms and training, and new domain names all in an effort to get clients. I had no previous marketing training and although my superpower was clear to me, I was not talking about it in a way that other people - the people who are seeking my particular magic - could understand.

So I did what any passionate empathic entrepreneur with a purpose would do. I got me some *hustle and grind.*

Over the course of 20 months I spent nearly $50,000.00 on the hustle and grind way of entrepreneurship. It did not work. I was scared and stressed. I struggled to provide the most basic needs for me and my animals. I didn't know it then but I do now that, I had to hit this "rock bottom" in order to heal my wounds around money.

You see, I have another soul wound. It's directly related to money. All the years I've worked for myself, from being a call girl, a Realtor, a massage therapist and yoga teacher, to being a coach and speaker the wound inhibiting my money making magic was, "I'm a piece of poor white trash."

This is how I got my money magic back.

BROKE

We're not broken, our beliefs are. When I realized that everything changed. I started to see how I was *not* my business or beliefs. I was able to detach myself (really, my self-worth) from them and focus on what I am here to create.

I was able to direct my energy to the gift I was born with and generate a positive outcome despite being broke AF.

Too many of us tie our worth to our work. Or to money.

We think that if we fail or fall short that means *we* are a failure. It's just not true. We let the source of our success be determined by how much money we're making. I'm not saying money isn't important. I'm suggesting that money is no the sole measure of success.

Earlier I said I was at rock bottom financially. The funny thing is I was a success at the exact same time. I was dealing with a lot of stress and fear of losing my home and yet, somehow I was not drunk by noon everyday.

I was not numbing the discomfort. I was not distracting myself with meaningless sex or social media or sleeping the day away.

I was responsible.

What I mean by that is I was able to respond *effectively* to a situation that would've shut me the fuck down before. I was responsible for my magic. I was able to stay connected to the truth of who I am rather than believing the soul wound story. I was writing a new story, telling a new truth about who I am and what I'm capable of - even if a mound of evidence might say otherwise.

I was broke financially but the richest I've ever been emotionally.

Instead of letting fear and shame send me down into the dark hole of suck, I used the 4 steps to heal myself. I realized that I am not "an ugly disgusting waste of time and piece of poor white trash" and remembered that *I am a beautiful magnetic woman that people love to be with. I am here to help my fellow empaths unmask their magic and be the badasses they were born to be.* I remembered the truth.

I then let that lead me. I woke up every day with that truth on my lips like a soothing lavender lip balm and would say it out loud as soon as I got up. I started the day with a "HELL YES, I CAN!" and so I did.

MY STORY: Badass Empath United

Like a phoenix, Badass Empath United was born out of the ashes of my rock bottom. I know I had to go there to get here.

Before I tell you where BE U (short for Badass Empath United) is today, allow me to take you back in time before she was even born. On Saturday, March 18, 2017 I wrote the following words in my journal.

6 Month Vision.

It's September 2017 and I am sitting on my back patio here at Bentwood. I am 100% at ease. I am filled with joy and abundance. Miracle after miracle has occurred in the area of finances for me. My money shit has been dealt with. Income is certain. I am generating $20,000.00 or more month after month after month now. I have a sold out group program, an online course that brings in revenue every day, and I am consistently enrolling 3 or 4 new VIP clients every month.

I am so satisfied with what I have created and I am overjoyed that I have become the woman in my vision.

I stripped down to build up.

It starts right now.

September arrived and I was nowhere near achieving this goal. In fact, it was that September that everything changed for me. In the 20 or so months leading up to it I was in hustle and grind mode. I was working harder than I ever have in my life. I had completely stopped going to yoga, was barely in the gym, and was eating whatever was fast and easy. I was so far off center that I hated what I was doing and cried most days (and nights) just praying things would fucking work.

Like I said earlier, I had made big investments, was all in, and had all the tools and training I needed to succeed but I was failing. Miserably.

The only thing I could do at that point was surrender.

Wednesday, September 6, 2017 was a full moon. I have a bathing ritual that I enjoy on new and full moons. There's a portal in my bathtub so my connection to Source, my Guides, and any other cosmic energy is enhanced on these days in this sacred place of mine. Across from the toilet.

On this full moon I bathed, listened to an energy clearing YouTube and "downloaded new programming." The most compelling thing that came through that night was this: "success and financial wealth only come from hard work" *is a myth.*

I know it's a super popular one that a lot of people buy into but I remembered otherwise that night. I knew better before, but I got caught up in the hype of the hustle and grind that most entrepreneurs get sucked into. Don't get me wrong, I know that it works for some. "Work harder. Longer hours. Self-sacrifice." These all serve some people well. Not my people. Not me.

The challenge, then, after that full moon download was that it was going against my "all-in" way of being that I thought would lead to consistent clients and profitability. So what should I do? Just stop? Give up? Throw in the towel?

Kinda. Ya.

I didn't give up on my business, however, I gave up on the belief that the only way to make it was through *hard work*.

Instead of going back to the drawing board (for the 13th time) and creating another webinar sales funnel, I turned my attention to mySelf. I asked, "What needs my love and attention right now?"

The answer I heard was, "The little girl who thinks nothing she does is good enough or everything is a disappointment. The feelings of oppression and fear and helplessness have been stirred. Looking at my life at 42 and where I'm at in my career crushes my spirit. *That's* why I'm depressed and nothing is working!"

The journaling continued.

> And this fucking tumor. It's HIM. It's dad. He's still keeping me quiet and small and afraid. Afraid of being seen and heard. Afraid of singing out loud. Afraid of making a statement, of being powerful.
>
> I'm still hiding out in my room.
> I'm still swallowing my pain.
> I'm still biting my tongue.
> I'm still holding it in.
> I'm still keeping quiet.
> I'm still tolerating disappointment.
> I'm still settling for less than I desire.
> I'm still suffering.
>
> I want to feel and be HAPPY.

I want to be successful and SAFE.

I want to TRUST men.

I want to be LOVE.

I want to take better care of myself.
I want to leave the house more.
I want to be consistent in my biz.
I want to be a better friend.
I want to to have great sex.
I want to watch less tv.
I want to go to yoga.
I want to make 10x more money.
I want to write a best-selling book.
I want to have a full client roster.

Writing this helped my see what there was to give up. Fear. The fear of being fully seen, fucking up or failing if I put myself all the way out there. I was holding back the part of me that is the most magical. I was hiding my weirdo. I was hiding the witchy side of me that could see and feel and know things. The "not normal" in me was afraid I would be rejected and ridiculed, just like I was when I was a little girl.

I kept the weirdo witchy woman hidden for years. I thought no one would take me seriously as a business owner if they knew my secret. But what I realized is my sensitivity and ability to perceive information that isn't material in form was actually my superpower.

My Guides said, "You're going to get what you want when you heal your soul wound. You will help others like you heal by seeing their wounds and holding the unwavering intention for them to succeed. You will feel the emotions with them so they can safely navigate all the uncomfortable stuff. You will speak the truth about what you see and feel and they will choose what to do with that information. Together, you will turn your dreams into reality, bring your visions to life. Your job, Colette, is to expose your superpower - the weirdo/witch - and use your gift openly with more people."

I was like, "So what you're saying is I have to expose my *sensitivity*, the thing I've spent my whole life protecting from rejection and ridicule!?"

Guides were all, "Yep."

Fuck. Talk about surrender.

From this state of surrender I had the absolute willingness to receive and be guided. I saw the path forward. I saw **Badass Empath United** - the next phase of my business. It was not intimacy-focused but people-focused. It didn't fit a formula. It fit *me*. Like a fucking glove. I am a badass empath and my sensitivity is my superpower. So is yours.

On Monday March 12, 2018 my big why became clear. I wrote:

> What's your why, Colette?
> Because I believe I am here to heal, to show people what's possible. I am here to be LOVE, MAGIC, and MIRACLES.
>
> Why is it important to be love, magic, and miracles?
> Because I feel the pain and suffering of all people.
> Because I can ease the suffering of others.
> Because I have the power to heal.
> Because the discomfort of numbing out has become more unbearable than tuning in.
> Because I want to feel love, and peace, and joy.
> Because I feel.

And so do my people. We feel everything more intensely. We

absorb fear and anger and shame. We take it in and hold onto it. We wall it off in our bodies. We get sick. We sacrifice ourselves to help others. We endure the suffering so they don't have to. And, we don't have to. I know how to safely release built up negative emotions, process the unwanted energy, and heal at a soul level.

I am an empath, healer, and teacher. I am here to help my people stop struggling and start trusting again so they can be the bight fucking light they are here to be.

Today BE U is booming! As 2018 came to an end I wrote this to acknowledge my hard work and commitment to being the badass I was born to be.

Saturday, December 22, 2018 (full moon in cancer)

What have I created this year?

- I've written 20 articles for empaths.

- I've written two e-books, one about confidence and one about intimacy.

- I created and launched Kick-Ass Confidence, an online course for empaths.

- I successfully launched a group course for healers, coaches, and holistic service providers to help them market their magic to the people who are hungry to hire them.

- I raised my coaching rates so I could start taking care of more than the minimums and live an abundant life.

- I supported 13 VIP coaching clients, helping them heal and transform their lives.

- I've spoken at three events, leading the audiences to more self-confidence so they can ask for and get what they want.

- I lead two workshops for women who want to connect to themselves and their partners more deeply.

- I had a single-day tantra retreat with a couple who came together to break through their long held patterns.

- I've hired a healer to help me free the lump.

- I've changed my lifestyle to support my physical healing.

- I've made numerous new friends, two of whom have become like sisters to me.

- I've become a leader in Society of WE, offering my time and guidance to members who are not as far along in their careers as I am.

- I hosted a dinner party for eight and got to share my love of cooking and entertaining with badass women.

- Most importantly, I healed myself at a soul level and am free to live with an open heart and a "Hell yes! I can" attitude.

I hope this personal story illustrates what's possible when we show up for ourselves. It's not easy. It's not normal. But when we do it, it's like winning the fucking lottery.

Chapter Five
SOUL LEVEL HEALING

Bad news: That horrible thing that happened? You called it to you.

Good news: We call forth such a crisis when we're truly ready to learn, heal, and grow.

A crisis is needed because it provokes our soul wound and stirs all the feelings associated with it. You know, the stuff we normally try to avoid. During a crisis we do one of two things, we either break down and stay down or we break down and *break through*. Breaking through means healing. So while the crisis itself sucks balls, it was necessary for your evolution. The breakthrough (healing) occurs when you're able to see the soul wound for what it is, you let yourself feel the feelings (instead of avoiding them), you reintegrate the cast-offs, and you restate the facts.

The things which hurt, instruct. - Benjamin Franklin

What is a Soul Wound?

Your soul wound is your greatest teacher. You received this unique-to-you wound when you were young so you could learn who you are, use your power to heal, and evolve as a human being. In more specific terms, a soul wound is a belief statement about who you are.

Think of it as an identity statement, an **"I am..." statement.** It's a disempowering, mean-as-hell identity statement that would make you cringe, cry, or punch somebody who called you that. Yep. It's not pretty. And there's a good reason for it.

The soul wound is buried pain inside of you that is waiting for your attention. It gets provoked when something upsetting happens.

The upset can be mild, like when someone you're into sends a text saying they're not into you and you feel rejected. Then there's the defcon-1 heartbreak situation when the person you love, and have given everything to, leaves you. Or maybe the upset is your childhood hood. Or your mom's denial and dissociative behavior. Or a tumor. You get the point.

All of these trigger events hit us in the heart-space. They hurt, but you don't have to let the pain linger.

The feelings of anger, betrayal, rejection, and powerlessness should be your focus in these situations. Your feelings, not the details of the situation, are the key points to help you overcome suffering and heal. These intense emotions are the indication that your soul wound has been provoked. If the pain weren't buried deep inside you already, you would not suffer at the hands of these circumstances.

The wound is where light enters you. - Rumi

What is YOUR Soul Wound?

I learned the following process from Jeffrey Van Dyk, an executive coach that works with leaders who feel a deep calling to help change our world on a global level. That's me. That's us.

Since I was eyeballs deep in soul wound healing work at the time, finding JVD and this process helped me to channel and organize the information I was receiving and make use of it. This simple process is concise, clean, and consistent in the results it generates. It is not, however, easy.

It is one of the most confronting and challenging things you will do.

If you're willing, it can be the pivotal point that turns your pain into purpose.

Use the following writing prompt to help you excavate *your soul wound*. Once you are able to 'be with' the wound, you no longer unconsciously shut down or strike back to avoid it. As a result, the wound can heal, and it no longer has to keep sabotaging your life.

Write down three of your most challenging events. One from early childhood, one from pre-teen and one from your teenage years. Next, for each experience, you will write answers to the five questions listed below. You can use the Magic Spell Book in chapter 8 to do this.

WHAT HAPPENED TO YOU?

This is the thing that happened that caused a reaction in you. It can be a trauma or something simple. Examples: I peed my pants in public. My dad ran over my mom with the Dodge. I was always afraid of getting yelled at by my angry father. My first boyfriend took the trash out and never came back.

WHAT DID YOU FEEL?

These are the emotions you felt related to the pain you experienced. Resist the urge to write about your stories here. Just make a list. Examples: I felt...stupid, out of control, hurt, sad, confused, angry, invisible, worthless, abandoned, betrayed, alone, embarrassed, rejected, hopeless, helpless, powerless, etc.

WHAT DID YOU LONG FOR?

These are the things you desperately wanted to feel. Think of them as your emotional needs. Again, just make a list. Examples: I longed to feel...safe, seen, loved, in control, held, validated, important, powerful, trust, acceptance, included, happy, hopeful, powerful, etc.

WHAT DID YOU DO TO COPE?

These are the things you did or became **in order to feel what you longed for.** When our emotional needs are not being met we cope in various ways to get them met. We learn how to get love and attention. Make a list. Example: Because I didn't want to get yelled at, I got all A's in school. (good girl) Because I was afraid of my dad, I hid in my room where it was safe. (small and silent) Because I felt ugly and disgusting, I became a call girl. (used my body to get attention) Because I was poor when I was young, I got a corvette when I was 21. (bought material things to feel important)

WHAT DID YOU TELL YOURSELF?

These are are the "I am statements" you made up about yourself when things happened at a young age. According to Jeffrey, "Wounding experiences are confusing, and when we're confused, we try to understand why something is happening, so we make up beliefs about ourselves and the world to make sense of what's happening. Essentially, we are saying 'oh, this is happening because I'm [fill in the blank]'; e.g., I'm unwanted, I'm broken, I'm unlovable, I'm a target, etc."

Take the last set of answers and compose your Soul Wound Statement. "I am...an ugly disgusting waste of time," for example. Keep writing it out until it hurts. Then you know you've hit it.

Now that you've uncovered your unique soul wound, get ready, it's about to get provoked. A lot.

In my experience taking clients through this wound excavating exercise it always brings up the shit you'd rather not feel. Your wound wants to stay hidden, lurking in the shadows of your mind, keeping you sick, small, sad, lonely, and broke. What a dick, right?

You will get triggered but you don't have to numb out, fight back, shut down, or lash out if you use the following four steps to heal yourself.

The 4 Steps to Breakthrough

Handling an emotional crisis leads to greater wisdom and results in lifetime benefits. Fear of life is really the fear of emotions. It is not the facts that we fear but our feelings about them. Once we have mastery over our feelings, our fear of life diminishes.— Dr. David R. Hawkins, Letting Go: The Pathway of Surrender

Emotional intelligence is the key to a kick-ass life.

When we can *be with* our emotions, rather than fight or fear them, we can then be in any situation and remain steady. Remaining steady (or fully present) isn't normal.

More often, when triggered, we shut down or strike back. In his book, *Power vs. Force*, Dr. Hawkins presents a scientific way to measure energy in the body. He provides a chart with levels of consciousness, emotional states, and life views.

In the early years of my healing journey, I descended from anger to fear to apathy, all of which are below the threshold of power. There's no way I could've cured my condition in those vibrational states. I had to dig deep into the emotional wounding (I know, it's ugly in there) and heal at a soul level if I was ever going to be free of Lumpy.

Heads up. Soul-level healing isn't an easy thing to do. It ain't pretty and it's not for everyone. It requires an investigation of all our deepest, darkest demons. In other words, we gotta deal with our shit. For real. But the payoff that comes from gettin' dirty and doing the deeper work is like winning the fucking lottery.

Here's how we do it.

SEE IT FOR WHAT IT IS.

The situation is not the issue. Your soul wound is what's causing you to shut down.

Over Christmas my soul wound was provoked when my brother, Clayton, berated me for not coming to a surprise housewarming party for my mom when she got the new trailer. So what allowed me to stay present and not run out of the room bawling my eyes out? I could see the situation for what it was. That was the first time in my life I could see it *in the moment.* I talk about and practice this stuff all the time, my business is built on teaching it, so don't expect yourself to have this advanced skill level right away.

What you could aim for is the ability to reflect on the triggering event and see it for what it was. The thing that happened, whatever it was, is not the issue. The person or people involved are not the issue. *Your response to the shit that happened is.*

If whatever happened made you shut down or strike back, that's all the indication you need to know your soul wound was provoked.

FEEL THE FEELINGS ASSOCIATED WITH THE WOUND.

As mentioned above, *the feelings* are the keys to healing. Normally, we attempt to avoid the uncomfortable feelings or sensations in our body. We do things to numb them like watch tv, eat comfort foods, drink, smoke, take drugs, and so on.

I'm suggesting we lean into them instead. Try this. When you're triggered, sit still (or walk around depending on the energy you're feeling) and tune your awareness to your body. Where do you feel the sensation? Try describing it either out loud or in a journal.

Talk to the feeling. *Yes, for real.*

Here's an example of what I mean. Let's say I got that text from the guy I was excited about dating. My soul wound, that includes fear of rejection, had me feeling anxiety.

I felt it in my gut.

I asked it, "What is this feeling?"

The answer was fear and disappointment.

Then I asked, "What are you telling me?"

The answer, "I'm not good enough"...or more specifically, "I'm an ugly, disgusting waste of time."

When you get to that deep pain, you know you've hit your wound.

From here, you can see the wound for what it is and process the pain quickly, healing yourself.

This process usually takes a loving guide to help you through but once you get it, your power returns. You are no longer at the mercy of your emotions - or other people's actions.

CALL BACK THE CAST-OFFS.

Wholeness is not achieved by cutting off a portion of one's being, but by integration of the contraries. - Carl Jung

Once you've softened the intensity of the pain (anger, anxiety, fear, etc) by feeling it and assessing its purpose you're better able to begin reclaiming the parts of you formerly cast off, or as Carl Jung says, "the contraries." What about yourself did you think was "ugly" or "disgusting"? Love those parts.

For instance, if you hated your feet give them your heart-felt attention and affection. If you're pissed at yourself for making the same mistake again and again, *calling yourself stupid*, now is the time to be kind. Now is the time to recognize that you *and only you* can give yourself the love you long for from the other person.

Try to investigate the rest of your soul wound. It's there to teach you how to return to wholeness so whatever you've deemed unworthy about yourself, it's time to embrace it and reintegrate it. Think about the word "healed", it's related to the word "whole" and "holy". Your wound is a spiritual one. Part of your spiritual journey is to love yourself unconditionally. And by that, I mean you gotta get down with the parts of you that you think are ugly, disgusting, and all-together unlovable and LOVE THE SHIT OUT OF THEM.

RESTATE THE FACTS.

Here's the part where you get to reprogram your beliefs about yourself. The soul wound comes with an attached story. The story is something you told yourself about yourself as a child and you have believed it to be true and factual all these years, subconsciously of course. Don't you think it's high time you put that bitch of a belief to bed and restate the facts? I'll use my lovely wound to demonstrate.

"I'm an ugly, disgusting waste of time." That's some pretty harsh shit. And it's been a subconscious belief (aka buried pain) impacting my conscious thoughts and behaviors since childhood. As a woman on a mission to heal myself and help others do the same, it would certainly be more productive to have powerful (not painful) subconscious beliefs. Restating the facts and reminding myself of the *real truth* is one way to do that. Here's what I'm going with: "I'm a beautiful magnetic woman people love to be with."

Ok. Your turn. Use these four steps to turn your crisis into gold. I believe this is how we heal our wounds and become the powerful, creative, loving creatures we're capable of being. If each of us accepted individual responsibility for our own well-being, joy and ability to love, imagine what our relationships would be like. Imagine what our world would be like.

That possibility is what drives me to continuously develop myself and help my clients *get their magic back*. For those of us who seek learning, healing, and growth we oftentimes get stuck on the HOW. My suggestion is to figure out the WHAT first. *What* is the emotion that gets triggered when something happens? *What* is your unique soul wound? *What* parts of you have you deemed unlovable? That's the place to focus your healing energy on.

Once you make a decision, the universe conspires to make it happen. - Ralph Waldo Emerson

Chapter Six
POWER UP!

Empaths fight with our feelings more than we flow with them. That's nuts.

Even more crazy is the internal dialogue, the made up (often negative) voice in our heads, is running the show. There are three main things we feelers need in order to navigate this reality effectively: rock solid healthy boundaries, an effective energy processing system that strengthens our emotional intelligence, and clear communication.

Boundaries

Daring to set boundaries is about having the courage to love ourselves even when we risk disappointing others.
- Brene Brown

Please stop talking about the need to *protect yourself* and instead start standing in your power. Clarify and honor your boundaries and you won't need the 'bubble of light.'

There's a fundamental flaw in the guidance most well-meaning teachers offer to empaths and highly sensitive people. The idea that we need to protect ourselves from other people's negative energy suggests we are incapable of handling it. It implies we are helpless victims. I don't buy it and neither should you. That stance reinforces the story that we are "too sensitive" or "too much." It weakens our resolve and has us *hiding out* (in some fucking bubble) instead of coming out as the super-humans we actually are.

So what can we do to strengthen our will, build our confidence, and be the badasses we were born to be?

The first thing we must do is see ourselves as capable. We cannot let society or our fears dictate who we are and how we show up. We get to choose. We can sit down, stay quiet and play small or we can stand up, be bold, and get to work having the kind of life we truly want.

Once we have a powerful perspective then healthy boundaries can be set.

Do you sometimes get easily overwhelmed - even though life is good? As empaths, we feel all the things. Unless we have the tools to handle our empathic abilities, we can get easily distressed. A good place to start is with our boundaries.

A boundary is a limit or space between you and the other person or situation. Healthy boundaries are set to make sure you are stable both mentally and emotionally. Setting boundaries can help empaths make decisions based on what is best for our unique sensitivities. This autonomy is an important part of our self-care and ability to show up fully in our lives. Here are a few of the specific ways having solid *healthy* boundaries will keep you from going over the edge (and beating yourself up at night).

FEELING POWERFUL

Personal boundaries help us decide what types of communication, behavior, and interaction are acceptable.

We feel powerful when we call the shots in our lives. By contrast, without boundaries, empaths who really just want other people to feel good, can give our power to them and/or the situation. That just makes us regretful, resentful, and causes us to retreat or retaliate. Not healthy. Not badass.

CONSISTENTLY HIGH VIBRATIONAL

Let's be honest, low vibes suck. And since we feel energy exponentially, we run like hell from the 'negative' emotions we feel. This is a bad news - good news situation.

The bad news is we cannot avoid the low vibe (negative) emotions. We must feel them to release them. If we try to avoid them they just get stuck in our bodies and turn into dis-ease. You probably have some of that going on right now. In other words, your magic might be missing in the area of health.

The good news is, once you allow yourself to fully feel and release those emotions (using the 4 steps from last chapter) you will have greater access to the high vibe ones. Hooray! Having healthy boundaries in place will make this whole *feeling thing* way less painful and easy to manage.

TRUSTING YOURSELF (AND OTHERS)

There's such a thing as having too rigid or unhealthy boundaries. Rigid boundaries mean we are likely to avoid intimacy and close relationships. We have a hard time asking for help. We end up very protective (always looking for the negative) and detached, even from romantic partners. The way to shift from rigid to healthy boundaries is to examine your wounds. When we avoid our soul wounds, slapping a numbing salve on them instead of healing them, we end up isolated and addicted.

However, I speak from experience when I say, "The wound is the way," and healing that shit is life changing. That's the whole purpose of this book, if ya hadn't noticed. Want to feel like you can trust yourself and others? Want to be at ease around people? Want to connect deeply without fear of rejection and have the kind of love you've always wanted? Do the soul wound work.

Listen, trust is a huge issue for us. I get it. Use this book to heal it. When we're healed and in state of wholeness, we find ourselves more confident than ever. That, my friend, is what I want for you.

SKYROCKETING SELF ESTEEM

Healthy boundaries protect our sense of self-esteem and ability to separate our feelings from others'. You know very well what it's like to absorb other people's thoughts, words and energy - it leaves you feeling depleted, confused, and doubting yourself. When our boundaries are intact, we are confident about who we are and what we want. We value our own opinions and we do not compromise our values. We can say 'no' and not feel bad about it.

"No" is a complete sentence. - Anne Lamott

So where do solid healthy boundaries come from? They come from out values. Here is an exercise to help you clarify your values.

Values Exercise

The following list of values will help you develop a clear sense of what's most important to you. Simply mark the values which most resonate with you, and then sort your list in order of priority. As you scan the values list below, you may find that while most values have little or no significance to you (and some may even seem negative to you), there are those values that just jump out and call to you, and you feel, "Yes, this value is part of me." This values list is merely a guide. It is lengthy and contains many synonyms but is certainly not exhaustive, so feel free to add unlisted values to your own list as well.

Abundance	Assertiveness	Carefulness
Acceptance	Assurance	Celebrity
Accessibility	Attentiveness	Certainty
Accomplishment	Attractiveness	Challenge
Accuracy	Audacity	Charity
Achievement	Availability	Charm
Activeness	Awareness	Chastity
Adaptability	Awe	Cheerfulness
Adoration	Balance	Clarity
Adroitness	Beauty	Cleanliness
Adventure	Being the best	Clear-mindedness
Affection	Belonging	Cleverness
Affluence	Benevolence	Closeness
Aggressiveness	Bliss	Comfort
Agility	Boldness	Commitment
Alertness	Bravery	Compassion
Altruism	Brilliance	Completion
Ambition	Buoyancy	Composure
Amusement	Calmness	Concentration
Anticipation	Camaraderie	Confidence
Appreciation	Candor	Conformity
Approachability	Capability	Congruency
Articulacy	Care	Connection

Consciousness
Consistency
Contentment
Continuity
Contribution
Control
Conviction
Conviviality
Coolness
Cooperation
Cordiality
Correctness
Courage
Courtesy
Craftiness
Creativity
Credibility
Cunning
Curiosity
Daring
Decisiveness
Decorum
Deference
Delight
Dependability
Depth
Desire
Determination
Devotion
Devoutness
Dexterity
Dignity
Diligence
Direction
Directness
Discipline
Discovery
Discretion

Diversity
Dominance
Dreaming
Drive
Duty
Dynamism
Eagerness
Economy
Ecstasy
Education
Effectiveness
Efficiency
Elation
Elegance
Empathy
Encouragement
Endurance
Energy
Enjoyment
Entertainment
Enthusiasm
Excellence
Excitement
Exhilaration
Expectancy
Expediency
Experience
Expertise
Exploration
Expressiveness
Extravagance
Extroversion
Exuberance
Fairness
Faith
Fame
Family
Fascination

Fashion
Fearlessness
Ferocity
Fidelity
Fierceness
Firmness
Fitness
Flexibility
Flow
Fluency
Focus
Fortitude
Frankness
Freedom
Friendliness
Frugality
Fun
Gallantry
Generosity
Gentility
Giving
Grace
Gratitude
Gregariousness
Growth
Guidance
Happiness
Harmony
Health
Heart
Helpfulness
Heroism
Holiness
Honesty
Honor
Hopefulness
Hospitality
Humility

Humor
Hygiene
Imagination
Impact
Impartiality
Independence
Industry
Ingenuity
Inquisitiveness
Insightfulness
Inspiration
Integrity
Intelligence
Intensity
Intimacy
Intrepidness
Introversion
Intuition
Intuitiveness
Inventiveness
Investing
Joy
Judiciousness
Justice
Keenness
Kindness
Knowledge
Leadership
Learning
Liberation
Liberty
Liveliness
Logic
Longevity
Love
Loyalty
Majesty
Mastery

Maturity
Meekness
Mellowness
Meticulousness
Mindfulness
Modesty
Motivation
Mysteriousness
Neatness
Nerve
Obedience
Open-mindedness
Openness
Optimism
Order
Organization
Originality
Outlandishness
Outrageousness
Passion
Peace
Perceptiveness
Perfection
Perkiness
Perseverance
Persistence
Persuasiveness
Philanthropy
Piety
Playfulness
Pleasantness
Pleasure
Poise
Polish
Popularity
Potency
Power
Practicality

Pragmatism
Precision
Preparedness
Presence
Privacy
Proactivity
Professionalism
Prosperity
Prudence
Punctuality
Purity
Realism
Reason
Reasonableness
Recognition
Recreation
Refinement
Reflection
Relaxation
Reliability
Religiousness
Resilience
Resolution
Resolve
Resourcefulness
Respect
Rest
Restraint
Reverence
Richness
Rigor
Sacredness
Sacrifice
Sagacity
Saintliness
Sanguinity
Satisfaction
Security

Self-control
Selflessness
Self-reliance
Sensitivity
Sensuality
Serenity
Service
Sexuality
Sharing
Shrewdness
Significance
Silence
Silliness
Simplicity
Sincerity
Skillfulness
Solidarity
Solitude
Soundness
Speed
Spirit
Spirituality
Spontaneity
Spunk
Stability
Stealth
Stillness
Strength

Structure
Success
Support
Surprise
Sympathy
Synergy
Teamwork
Temperance
Thankfulness
Thoroughness
Thoughtfulness
Thrift
Tidiness
Timeliness
Tranquility
Transcendence
Trust
Truth
Unflappability
Uniqueness
Unity
Understanding
Usefulness
Utility
Variety
Victory
Vigor
Virtue

Vision
Vitality
Vivacity
Warmth
Watchfulness
Wealth
Willingness
Winning
Wisdom
Wittiness
Wonder
Youthfulness
Zeal

Let's narrow it down now. What are your top 5 values? (ex. love, freedom, self-expression, etc.)

1.
2.
3.
4.
5.

For each value, write out a boundary statement. (ex. I align myself with love. I will not stay where I feel stuck - in a relationship or stage of life. I will not sacrifice my self-expression to "fit in," etc.)

1.

2.

3.

4.

5.

Use these statements to stay aware of how you're responding to people and situations. When a boundary is being crossed, by you or someone else, you can recognize it and make an informed decision on how to proceed. You will get your magic back when you know, honor, and communicate your boundaries well.

Emotional Intelligence

Currently not letting anybody fuck with my flow. — unknown

You already know the four steps to processing unproductive energy and emotion.

1. See it for what it is.

2. Feel the feelings associated with it.

3. Call back the cast-offs.

4. Restate the facts.

So let's talk more specifically about emotional intelligence. Your success processing the energy you feel when you're triggered depends on how well you understand your emotions. Oh how I wish they taught us this in school but they don't. Which is why you're shutting down or striking back when shit happens.

The following EQ chart is derived from Dr. David R. Hawkins' book, *Power vs. Force*. Understanding the full range of human emotions and how their corresponding energy affects you (and others) is vital to living an extraordinary life.

Enlightenment
This is the highest level of human consciousness where one has become like God. Many see this as Christ, Buddha, or Krishna. These are those who have influenced all of mankind.

Peace
Peace is achieved after a life of complete surrender to the Creator. It is where you have transcended all and have entered that place that Dr. Hawkins calls illumination. Here, a stillness and silence of mind is achieved, allowing for constant revelation. Only 1 in 10 million people will live at this level.

Joy
With unconditional Love, there follows a constant accompaniment of true happiness. No personal tragedy or world event could ever shake someone living at this level of consciousness. They seem to inspire and lift all those who come in contact with them. They have enormous patience and a relentlessly positive attitude.

Love
Only if, in the level of Reason, you start to see yourself as a potential for the greater good of mankind, will you have enough power to enter here. Here is where you start applying what was learned in your reasoning and you let the heart take over rather than the mind - you live by intuition. This is the level of compassion - a selfless love that has no desire except for the welfare of those around them. It is UNCONDITIONAL.

Reason
The level of science, medicine, and a desire for knowledge. Your thirst for knowledge becomes insatiable. You don't waste time in activities that do not provide educational value. Paradoxically, Reason can become a stumbling block for further progressions of consciousness and can keep you from intimate connection with others.

Acceptance
If Courage is the realization that you are the source of your life's experiences, then it is here where you become the creator of them. You begin to awaken your potential through action. Here's where you begin to set and achieve goals and to actively push yourself beyond your previous limitations. Here's where you turn things around, take control, and become proactive.

Willingness
You see life as one big possibility. No longer are you satisfied with complacency - you strive to do your best at whatever task you've undertaken. You begin to develop self-discipline and willpower and learn the importance of sticking to a task till the end.

Neutrality
Neutrality is the level of flexibility. You are unattached to outcomes. At this level, you are satisfied with your current life situation. You are capable of non judgemental appraisal of problems. You realize the possibilities but don't make the sacrifices required to reach a higher level.

Courage
This is the level of empowerment. It is the first level where you are not taking life energy from those around you. This empowerment leads you to the realization that you alone are in charge of your own growth and happiness.

Pride
Since the majority of people are below this point, this is the level that most aspire to. In comparison to Shame and Guilt, one begins to feel positive here. However, it's a false positive. It's dependent upon external conditions such as wealth, position or power.

Anger
As one moves out of Apathy to Grief and then out of Fear, they begin to want. Desire which is not fulfilled leads to frustration which brings us to Anger. Anger can be constructive or destructive - depending on how it is expressed.

Desire
Desire is a major motivator for much of our society. Although desire can be an impetus for change, the downside is that it leads to enslavement to ones appetites. This is the level of addiction to such things as sex, money, prestige, or power.

Fear
This is the emotional state of most of the world. Suspicion and defensiveness are common. People become obsessed with feeling "safe" and are unable to grow as individuals.

Grief
Many of us have felt this at times of tragedy in our lives. However, having this as your primary emotional state, you live a life of constant regret and remorse. This is the level where you feel all your opportunities have passed you by. You ultimately feel you are a failure.

Apathy
The level of hopelessness and despair. At this level, one has resigned themselves to their current situation and feels numb to life around them.

Guilt
Feelings of worthlessness and an inability to forgive oneself are common here. Guilt is used to punish ourselves and manipulate others, and is a symptom of victimhood.

Shame
At this level, people are constantly exposed to the vulnerability of other "negative" emotions. This is the lowest vibrational state we feel. As such, we hide the hurt hoping no one will see how bad we are. But we are not our emotions. *We* are not shameful. Shame is something we feel when we've done something we consider to be wrong or morally unacceptable.

Just like you can't control the weather, you cannot "control your emotions". So stop trying to. Instead, become aware of them. Stop avoiding the uncomfortable ones, too. The extent to which you avoid them is the same extent to which you will be unable to feel those you want - like Love, Joy, and Peace. While there are some emotions that don't feel good in our bodies (Shame, Guilt, Grief, Fear) that does not make them "bad" or "wrong". Think about the weather. There are conditions we don't often care for but they are a part of our experience on earth. Calling a rainstorm "bad weather" is simply an opinion. A farmer dependent on the rain sees it differently. The point is, as humans, we have emotions and you can expect to experience the full range.

Instead of asking yourself "Why do I feel this way?" (the answer, btw, is because you're human) ask yourself "What information is this emotion bringing me?" Get good at this and you will no longer be at the mercy of your emotions. Where you hang out - your primary emotional state - is a matter of your self-awareness and conscious choice. As you grow, your consciousness evolves and your primary emotional state elevates.

Try this. Think of something right now that you feel guilty about. We all have something! Now investigate the story in your mind. Can you call forth the forgiveness and Love needed to free yourself of that self-induced punishment? Keep going until you can! Then ask yourself the deeper question - what information was this emotion bringing me? And what is there to do about it now?

With this awareness in place, we can then step up our communication skills. Being able to speak our truth to other people is necessary if we want satisfying relationships.

Clear Communication

To effectively communicate, we must all realize we are different in the way we perceive the world and use this as a guide to our communication with others. — Tony Robbins

You know how sometimes self-doubt creeps in - even though you know in your gut what's right? Being an empath means we know things intuitively. The problem arises when we don't say anything. We have this bad habit of staying silent because we don't want to come across too smart, or too needy, or too emotional, or too weird. We'd rather bite our tongue than be accused of being too sensitive again.

Here's the thing. It doesn't do anyone any good when we shut down or stay small. There is a way to effectively communicate what we feel (and know) that allows a caring partner or family member or colleague to hear it without negatively reacting. It's up to us to lead that aspect of the relationship. Most people are not empaths, which means your partner, family, and business associates may not have ever had to relate to a highly sensitive, intuitive, magical person. Also, non-empaths may feel intimidated or even threatened by our 'powers'. They don't always know what to do with us. So we need to lead with compassion and clear, confident communication.

The last thing I want for you or your partner is to pull away from from each other because of shitty communication. Being an intimacy expert for 25 years has revealed to me that poor communication is the number one reason couples fight. I'm here to tell ya, effective communication can be learned.

Spider-Man said it best, "With great power comes great responsibility." Empaths have "abnormal abilities" and we need to get responsible for them. That means being kick-ass-confident with our boundaries, emotional intelligence, and communication.

HEAD VS. HEART

Did you know your communication can either be ego-based or love-based, but not both at the same time? This is good news. And I'll tell you what I mean, but first let me describe the difference.

Ego-based communication is full of judgment, expectation, and really only allows for a narrow perspective. Oftentimes control and the 'fight to be right' come from this place. By contrast, heart-based communication is loving and cooperative. You're able to be present and see other points of view. And really, you're communicating in an effort to understand and connect. The problem is most people hang out in their heads, where ego resides. So when communicating, there's an unconscious drive to be right. This creates the need to control and that behavior is a pain in everyone's ass.

Married gals, when you act this way with your partner, it implies he's not capable and leaves him feeling kind of worthless. Has your husband stopped trying? Guess what? It may be because you've taught him to be that way. Have you ever said something like this to your man: "You know what? I asked you to do this last week and it's still not done, so never mind. I should've known I'd have to do it myself."

But what you didn't say out loud is, "What the fuck? Is he completely useless? It's like I'm his mother. ARHG!"

I thought so.

So here's the thing, you are not alone. And it's not your fault. This goes for everyone, you either haven't learned high-level communication skills or you're having trouble putting them into action because you haven't dealt with the resentment. Or even more likely, you have not healed your soul wound.

Let's look at how to get out of your head and into your heart.

First, take inventory. Right now, where are you? Are you in resistance, fighting to be right? Or are you open and receptive and generous with your listening? Take a breath, a deep releasing breath. Let your awareness drop into your heart. Feel, look, or a listen for the truth that resides there, for the love and commitment you want to honor.

Now imagine the possibility of being calm and clear and able to say what's in your heart. You can tell your truth, you trust yourself, and you're openly expressing your heart's desire. You're free from hesitation, from fear, and you're even receptive to the other person's response. No more shutting down. Even better, no more striking back.

Great communication happens when you get out of your head and get into your heart. Honor your values and boundaries.. Express your truth and allow him (or whoever you're struggling to communicate with) to as well. If you can do this one thing today – do it! It will make a huge difference. I promise.

Here is a suggested action item for you.

Share what you've learned from this book with someone. As you're getting ready to open up, breathe deeply. And notice if you're in your head or your heart. You can always use the breath to shift from ego to love.

Chapter Seven
NOW WHAT?

Well now you have some tools at your fingertips to help you heal your soul wound. I wrote this book for empaths and highly sensitive people who want to stop struggling and start trusting again. But if it were as easy as reading a book to heal yourself and transform your life, we'd all be enlightened. Unfortunately, information does not equal implementation.

For empaths and HSPs when we struggle with health, money, or love, our gift feels more like a curse. Our emotional sensitivity can cause us to shut down super quick. Do that enough times and you lose your gift. When we've lost our magic and are stuck in the muck it's hard to pull ourselves out on our own. So what I'd like you to consider now is getting support.

We are here to make a difference in the world. Whether you're an empathic parent raising conscious kids or a heart-based entrepreneur doing healing work or simply a sensitive person trying to get by in this world, it's vital we deal with the deeply buried emotional wounds so we can be the badasses we were born to be.

For too long, we have numbed out and dumbed down to fit in. Our differences make us uniquely capable of loving others but we build walls around our hearts to stay safe instead. We have the power to love and heal ourselves and others. It's time to own that magic. The world needs us to show up, deal with our shit, and get to work making *love, magic, and miracles* the new normal. If your current normal is more Struggle Boat than Love Boat and you want to jump ship then here's how I can help.

Get Your Magic Back
Free Your Heart, Find Your Voice,
Love Your Life

Stress, overwhelm, anxiety, depression, loneliness, and addiction are *not normal*. Some of us have even become so accustomed to living with these challenges that we don't know what it's like to be free. We don't have a reference point for feeling safe, supported, seen and fully satisfied. We only know life to be, in fact, a struggle. That shit just needs to stop. I created this program to help make it happen.

See if this resonates…

- You have magic inside of you, but instead of being a badass you're trying to be "normal".
- You have buried pain locked away in your body and you need to release the build up of negative emotions.
- You secretly harbor feelings of shame, fearing rejection or being found out.
- You have trust issues that keep you from fully connecting and having a truly satisfying intimate relationship.
- You can't seem to find your voice and speak your truth.
- You tend more toward self-sabotage than self-confidence.
- You are ready to break the patterns and habits that keep you stuck, stressed, and struggling.

- You're ready to be free of the mind-fuck!
- You want to go from chaos to clear and confident and you want it now.
- You want to stop getting triggered all the time.
- You want those old ass self-defeating stories to stop playing in your head.
- You want to face your health challenge head-on and know you're capable of conquering it this time.
- You want to fix your broken relationship(s) instead of blaming and fighting or ignoring them.
- You want to deal with your money shit and break the feast or famine pattern you've lived with your whole life.

If you're shaking your head yes to some (or most) of those I encourage you to apply for the Get Your Magic Back 10-week group program.

It is *the program* for empaths and HSPs who want to free their heart, find their voice, and love their life!

AS A RESULT OF THIS PROGRAM YOU WILL...

- **Release the top 3 things that are holding you back.** Clarify who you will BE, what you will DO, and what you will HAVE as a result of getting your magic back. Connect to your BIG WHY (soul's purpose).

- **Upgrade and organize your environment in order to achieve greatness.** Understand how internal and external environments will make or break your success. Get the tools to make it happen.

- **Excavate your soul wound with an experienced guide.** Learn what yours is, where it comes from and how it fucks with you. Safely dive into the deep end and start the healing process. Don't do it alone.

- **Implement the 4-step system for healing the soul wound in the real world.** First up, get control. Separate the situation that triggers you from the soul wound that sends you spiraling.

- **Master your sensitivities.** How to stop your numb out behavior when shit happens. Manage your emotions and finally be free.

- **Love yourself like your life depends on it.** Instantly reintegrate the "unlovable" parts of yourself so you can get on with living a kick ass life.

- **Write your new story.** Take your power back and heal yourself at a soul level. Begin working from a new, purpose-driven, operating system. Leave the wounded one behind.

- **Unmask your magic.** Take bold courageous action from the new operating system. Create a strategy for living a life that is magical AF.

- **Use your voice.** Learn how to fearlessly communicate your feelings, wants, and needs. Ask for and get what you really want - at work, at home, and from the Universe.

In less than three months you will transform *at a soul level*...so you can live your most kick-ass life.

I believe the world needs sensitive souls like us to be healthy and happy AF, doing work we love that makes a bunch of money so we can be a bright fucking light. *That is our magic.* If you agree and want to GET YOUR MAGIC BACK, with me as your guide, apply here: www.colettedavenport.com/get-your-magic-back

Chapter Eight
YOUR MAGIC SPELL BOOK

This is a magic spell book. Whatever is written in these pages gets created with Divine Energy and effortless ease.

Cast only spells that are for the greater good of all life. Only write in this book when you have love in your heart. Commune with the Guidance to get clear about what you are called to create. Once a spell has been cast, breathe a deep breath of surrender and trust that the forces are with you and already working to manifest your intentions.

And so it is.

And so it is.

And so it is.

_____

_____

_____

_____

_____

_____

_____

_____

_____

_____

_____

_____

_____

_____

_____

_____

_____

_____

_____

_____

_____

_____

_____

_____

_____

_____

_____

_____

_____

_____

_____

_____

_____

_____

_____

_____

_____

_____

_____

_____

_____

_____

_____

_____

_____

_____

_____

_____

_____

_____

_____

_____

_____

_____

_____

_____

_____

_____

_____

_____

_____

_____

_____

_____

_____

_____

_____

_____

_____

_____

_____

_____

_____

_____

_____

_____

_____

_____

_____

_____

_____

_____

_____

_____

_____

_____

_____

_____

_____

_____

_____

_____

_____

_____
_____
_____
_____
_____
_____
_____
_____
_____
_____
_____
_____
_____
_____
_____
_____
_____
_____
_____
_____
_____
_____

_____

_____

_____

_____

_____

_____

_____

_____

_____

_____

_____

_____

_____

_____

_____

_____

_____

_____

_____

_____

_____

_____

_____

_____

_____

_____

_____

_____

_____

_____

_____

_____

_____

_____

_____

_____

_____

_____

_____

_____

_____

_____

_____

_____

_____

_____

_____

_____

_____

_____

_____

_____

_____

_____

_____

_____

_____

_____

_____

_____

_____

_____

_____

_____

_____

_____

_____

_____

_____

_____

_____

_____

_____

_____

_____

_____

_____

_____

_____

_____

_____

_____

_____

_____

_____

_____

_____

_____

_____

_____

_____

_____

_____
_____
_____
_____
_____
_____
_____
_____
_____
_____
_____
_____
_____
_____
_____
_____
_____
_____
_____
_____
_____
_____
_____
_____
_____

_____

_____

_____

_____

_____

_____

_____

_____

_____

_____

_____

_____

_____

_____

_____

_____

_____

_____

_____

_____

_____

_____

_____

_____

_____

_____

_____

_____

_____

_____

_____

_____

_____

_____

_____

_____

_____

_____

_____

_____

_____

_____

_____

_____

_____

_____

_____

_____

_____

_____

_____

_____

_____

_____

_____

_____

_____

_____

_____

_____

_____

_____

_____

_____

_____

_____

_____

_____

_____

_____

_____

_____

_____

_____

_____

_____

_____

_____

_____

_____

_____

_____

_____

_____

_____

_____

_____

_____

_____

_____

_____

_____

_____

_____

_____

_____

_____

_____

_____

_____

_____

_____

_____

_____

_____

_____

_____

_____

_____

_____

_____

_____

_____

_____

_____

_____

_____

_____

_____

_____

_____

_____

_____

Remember…

YOU ARE
Magical AF

ABOUT THE AUTHOR

Colette Davenport is a Master Empath and CEO of Badass Empath United, a global organization that provides personal and professional development exclusively for empaths. She is an international coach, speaker, and workshop leader.

Colette's two decades of experience in the relationship field, along with her personal health crisis, and her fine tuned empathic abilities generated a unique vision for the future of the highly sensitive community. She believes empaths can only live up to their full potential through emotional mastery and speaking their truth. When this happens on a global scale, the world as we know it will shift from fear to love.

Made in the USA
Middletown, DE
11 December 2019